Weiss Ratings' Consumer Guide to Homeowners Insurance

Weiss Ratings' Consumer Guide to Homeowners Insurance

Fall 2017

GREY HOUSE PUBLISHING

Weiss Ratings
4400 Northcorp Parkway
Palm Beach Gardens, FL 33410
561-627-3300

Independent. Unbiased. Accurate. Trusted.

Published by Grey House Publishing, Inc., located at 4919 Route 22, Amenia, NY 12501; telephone 518-789-8700. Grey House Publishing neither guarantees the accuracy of the data contained herein nor assumes any responsibility for errors, omissions or discrepancies. Grey House Publishing accepts no payment for listing; inclusion in the publication of any organization, agency, institution, publication, service or individual does not imply endorsement of the publisher.

4919 Route 22
PO Box 56
Amenia, NY 12501-0056

Fall 2017 Edition

ISBN: 978-1-68217-443-2
ISSN: 2164-4187

CONTENTS

Terms and Conditions

This document is prepared strictly for the confidential use of our customer(s). It has been provided to you at your specific request. It is not directed to, or intended for distribution to or use by, any person or entity who is a citizen or resident of or located in any locality, state, country or other jurisdiction where such distribution, publication, availability or use would be contrary to law or regulation or which would subject Weiss Ratings, LLC or its affiliates to any registration or licensing requirement within such jurisdiction.

No part of the analysts' compensation was, is, or will be, directly or indirectly, related to the specific recommendations or views expressed in this research report.

This document is not intended for the direct or indirect solicitation of business. Weiss Ratings, LLC, and its affiliates disclaim any and all liability to any person or entity for any loss or damage caused, in whole or in part, by any error (negligent or otherwise) or other circumstances involved in, resulting from or relating to the procurement, compilation, analysis, interpretation, editing, transcribing, publishing and/or dissemination or transmittal of any information contained herein.

Weiss Ratings, LLC has not taken any steps to ensure that the securities or investment vehicle referred to in this report are suitable for any particular investor. The investment or services contained or referred to in this report may not be suitable for you and it is recommended that you consult an independent investment advisor if you are in doubt about such investments or investment services. Nothing in this report constitutes investment, legal, accounting or tax advice or a representation that any investment or strategy is suitable or appropriate to your individual circumstances or otherwise constitutes a personal recommendation to you.

The ratings and other opinions contained in this document must be construed solely as statements of opinion from Weiss Ratings, LLC, and not statements of fact. Each rating or opinion must be weighed solely as a factor in your choice of an institution and should not be construed as a recommendation to buy, sell or otherwise act with respect to the particular product or company involved.

Past performance should not be taken as an indication or guarantee of future performance, and no representation or warranty, expressed or implied, is made regarding future performance. Information, opinions and estimates contained in this report reflect a judgment at its original date of publication and are subject to change without notice. Weiss Ratings, LLC offers a notification service for rating changes on companies you specify. For more information visit WeissRatings.com or call 1-877-934-7778. The price, value and income from any of the securities or financial instruments mentioned in this report can fall as well as rise.

This document and the information contained herein is copyrighted by Weiss Ratings, LLC. Any copying, displaying, selling, distributing or otherwise delivering of this information or any part of this document to any other person or entity is prohibited without the express written consent of Weiss Ratings, LLC, with the exception of a reviewer or editor who may quote brief passages in connection with a review or a news story.

Weiss Ratings' Mission Statement

Weiss Ratings' mission is to empower consumers, professionals, and institutions with high quality advisory information for selecting or monitoring a financial services company or financial investment. In doing so, Weiss Ratings will adhere to the highest ethical standards by maintaining our independent, unbiased outlook and approach to advising our customers.

About This Guide

Everyone needs a place to live and a place to store their possessions. Whether you own a home or condominium or rent an apartment or room, you have a need to purchase homeowners or renters insurance. What most people don't realize, however, is that it is often very easy to save hundreds of dollars per year on homeowners insurance by simply educating yourself and shopping around.

This is where Weiss Ratings can help. This publication is designed to give you a good overview of your homeowners insurance options. It walks you through the considerations for selecting the appropriate type of insurance and coverage levels, plus it gives you instructions on how to find the best price from a strong, reputable insurer.

Best of all, you can rest assured that the information presented here is completely independent and free of bias. Weiss Ratings does not sell insurance, we are not connected with any insurance companies, and we won't make a single penny should you decide to purchase a policy from one of the companies listed in this guide. Our goal is to simply help you make the best decision possible - for you.

Anatomy of a Homeowners Insurance Policy

At its core, homeowners insurance is simply a contract between you and your insurance company to protect against financial loss in the unfortunate event that your home is damaged or your property is stolen. Depending on the property you own, the insurance coverage can provide financial assistance to:

- repair your home or rebuild it in the event it is damaged or destroyed;
- reimburse you for or replace items stolen from your home or vehicle; and
- pay for any medical expenses arising from injuries a guest to your home sustains while on your property.

Although there are no statutory requirements for homeowners insurance, most lenders require you to carry coverage at least equal to the amount of your outstanding mortgage.

Generally speaking, homeowners policies are defined by the causes of loss that they cover. The three definitions are basic, broad, and special. The basic causes of loss that are covered by homeowners policies are:

fire	lightning	windstorm
hail	explosion	riot or civil commotion
aircraft	vehicles	smoke
vandalism or malicious mischief	theft	volcanic eruption

The broad causes of loss include these basic ones listed above plus the following:

- falling objects
- weight of ice, sleet, or snow
- damage by broken window glass
- accidental discharge from a plumbing or heating system
- sudden and accidental tearing apart, cracking, burning, or building of a steam or hot water system
- freezing of plumbing or of a heating or air conditioning system

The special form is also called All-Risk and covers any cause of loss unless it is specifically excluded.

There are seven different standardized forms of coverage available. They are:

- HO-1 Basic Form
- HO-2 Broad Form
- HO-3 Special Form - most common for owner-occupied homes
- HO-4 Contents Broad Form - common coverage for tenants living in apartments
- HO-5 Comprehensive Form
- HO-6 Unit-Owners Form - usually purchased by condominium owners
- HO-8 Modified Coverage Form

HO-1 and HO-8 cover only the "basic" causes of loss. HO-2 covers the "broad" causes of loss. HO5 is very similar to the HO-3 homeowners policy except that it covers the special causes of loss on both the dwelling and personal property whereas the HO-3 form covers special causes of loss on the dwelling but the broad causes of loss on personal property.

Each policy is divided into five sections:

- Property Coverages
- Liability Coverages
- Additional Coverages
- Exclusions
- Conditions

PROPERTY COVERAGES

Insurance for Homeowners-Form HO-3

The form HO-3 homeowners policy includes five types of property coverages for the structures on your property and the possessions that you own. The homeowners policy is considered special coverage because it covers any cause of loss that is not specifically excluded. It is sometimes called an "all-risks" policy.

- **Coverage A and Coverage B - Dwelling and Other Structures** - These sections cover your house and any attached and unattached structures. There is also coverage under this section for any building materials or supplies located on your property for use in construction, alteration, or repair of buildings on your property. You decide the amount you want to cover your dwelling for, called "limit of coverage." When selecting this limit, remember that the insurance is for the building, not the land, so use the cost to replace your home as a guide rather than the market value. See your individual policy for specific limits and exclusions.

- **Coverage C - Personal Property** - This section provides coverage for your personal property anywhere in the world. The limit of coverage for this section is usually 50% of the dwelling amount. Personal property is covered on a cash value basis, but replacement cost is available. Special limits apply to some types of property and some property is excluded from coverage.

There are 11 types of property that are subject to special limits in this section of coverage. They are:

- $200 on money, bank notes, bullion, gold other than goldware, silver other than silverware, platinum other than platinumware, coins, medals, scrip, stored value cards and smart cards

- $1,500 on securities, accounts, deeds, evidences of debt, letters of credit, notes other than bank notes, manuscripts, personal records, passports, tickets and stamps.

- $1,500 on watercraft of all types, including their trailers, equipment and engines or motors.

- $1,500 on trailors or semitrailors not used with watercraft

- $1,500 for theft of jewelry, watches, furs, precious and semiprecious stones.

- $2,500 for theft of firearms and related equipment

- $2,500 for theft of silverware, silver-plated ware, goldware, gold-plated ware, platinumware, platinum-plated ware and pewterware.

- $2,500 for property on the premises used for business

- $500 for property away from the premises used for business. This does not apply to electronic apparatus as described in the next two items

- $1,500 on electronic apparatus and accessories while in a motor vehicle, but only if the apparatus is equipped to be operated with power from the motor vehicle.

- $1,500 on electronic apparatus and accessories used primarily for business while away from the premises and not in or upon a motor vehicle. The apparatus must be equipped to be operated by power from the motor vehicle.

If you own any of these items, you can have coverage added to your policy under a Scheduled Coverage endorsement, or you can purchase a separate policy called an Inland Marine policy. The property will be itemized on the policy and a limit will be attached. The property will probably be photographed or appraised. When you have these endorsements or policies, you are covered for more causes of loss and do not have to pay a deductible. Please talk to your agent or insurance company if you have any of these items that need to be scheduled.

- **Coverage D - Loss of Use -** This section provides money for additional living expenses in the event your home is uninhabitable after a loss. The limit of coverage is usually 20% of the dwelling amount. There are different ways of calculating the payment, so review your policy for your specific requirements and limits.

Insurance for Tenants - Form HO-4

The tenants policy does not include any Dwelling or Other Structures coverage since the tenant does not own, nor is responsible for any of the insurance on the building itself. The tenants policy is considered a "broad form" because it covers the basic causes of loss along with six other causes.

- **Coverage C - Personal Property -**This is the primary limit for the tenants coverage and provides the same coverage as the Coverage C of the Homeowners HO-3 policy (see above). Coverage is provided on an actual cash value basis, but replacement cost coverage may be available. In the event that you have made substantial alterations to a rented unit, you can purchase an endorsement that will cover these items.

  The normal coverage amount on this endorsement is 10% of the Coverage C limit, but higher limits may be purchased. Also, if you have a waterbed, landlords will sometimes ask you to carry insurance specifically for damage the bed may cause. There is an endorsement for this as well.

- **Coverage D - Loss of Use -** The limit of liability for this coverage is 20% of Coverage C, and coverage depends upon the covered causes of losses for Coverage C. See the description of Coverage D above for more information about Coverage D. See your policy for further information about the causes of loss covered under your policy.

Insurance for Unit Owners - Form HO-6

The unit owner's policy is very similar to the homeowners policy but only provides the coverages needed. Also, the unit owner's form lists the causes of loss it covers rather than what it excludes as the homeowners does. The policy is set up as follows:

- **Coverage A - Dwelling -** This coverage is separated into four categories. The limit is usually rather low since it covers all four categories, but can be increased and is provided on a replacement cost basis. You should check with your association to see if you need to provide coverage for any other areas.

  a. The first category includes the appliances, cabinets, and improvements that are part of the owners unit.
  b. The second category includes exterior items that are part of the residence, such as windows and patio doors.
  c. The third category includes any common area that the unit owner is responsible for.
  d. The fourth category covers any buildings that aren't attached to the unit such as a garage.

- **Coverage C - Personal Property** - This coverage is the same as Coverage C for a homeowners policy except that you select the limit based upon the value of your possessions rather than simply calculating it as a percentage of Coverage A. Coverage is provided on an actual cash value basis, but replacement cost coverage may be available.

- **Coverage D - Loss of Use** - This coverage is the same as with the homeowners policy except that the limit is 40% of Coverage C.

LIABILITY COVERAGES

This section of your policy includes two types of liability coverage: "personal liability" and "medical payments to others" and is the same on all forms of homeowners policies including the tenants form and the unit owners form.

- **Personal Liability** - This section covers injury and damage to property that the insurer is legally responsible for. For example, your dog bites a passerby, a neighbor is injured in your swimming pool, or your bathtub overflows into the apartment or unit below. The usual limit for this coverage is $100,000, but higher limits may be purchased. This section also covers your acts away from your home in the event you injure someone while golfing or hunting for example.

- **Medical Payments to Others** - This coverage pays for necessary medical expenses for injuries that occur on your property or in your unit. This is not health insurance for the insured or the insured's family members but attempts to avoid lawsuits by promptly paying for injuries from an accident that the insured may be responsible for. The limit for this coverage is generally $1,000.

ADDITIONAL COVERAGES

The following coverages are included in the standard homeowners policy, with certain limitations. The coverages on the tenants and unit owners' policies are the same unless noted.

Property Coverages

- **Debris removal** - Coverage for reasonable expense for removal of debris (an example of a covered expense is the cost of removing damaged items from a home following a fire.). This coverage is included in the dwelling coverage limit.

- **Reasonable repairs** - Coverage for repairs made to a structure to prevent more damage.

- **Trees, shrubs and other plants** - Coverage for damage to trees. The limit for this coverage on a homeowners policy is 5% of the dwelling coverage but no more than $500 for one tree. The limit on a tenants policy is 20% of Coverage C. The limit on the unit owners policy is 10% of Coverage C.

- **Fire department service charge** - Coverage for up to $500 of service charges incurred when the fire department is called to your house.

- **Property removed** - Coverage for property that is removed from your home after the home is damaged. This is to protect you while storing your belongings in another location while your home is repaired or rebuilt.

- **Credit card, fund transfer card, forgery, and counterfeit money** - Coverage for up to $500 for theft or unauthorized use of your funds.

- **Loss assessment** - Coverage up to $1,000 for an assessment by your home owners association or condo owners association for damages.

- **Collapse** - Coverage is provided if your house collapses for various reasons.

- **Glass or safety glazing material** - Coverage for glass breakage and damage to property from the broken glass.

- **Landlord's furnishings** - Coverage up to $2,500 for loss to furnishings in an apartment or room in your home that you rent out. This is not included on the tenants or unit owners policies.

- **Additions and Alterations** - This is covered in Coverage A and B on the homeowners policy. Coverage is provided for improvements acquired at your expense (for example a new ceiling fan). The limit on the tenants policy is 10% of the Coverage C limit.

Liability Coverages

- **Claim expense -** This is coverage for the cost the insurance company incurs to defend you against a lawsuit. Included are costs of claims adjusters, defense attorneys, investigators and expert witnesses

- **First aid expense -** This is coverage for first aid to others incurred by an insured, but it does not apply to injuries of the insured. There is no limit to this coverage.

- **Damage to property of others -** Coverage for damage you cause to someone else's property up to $500 per occurrence.

- **Loss assessment -** Coverage up to $1,000 for an assessment by your home owners association or condo owners association for damages as a result of a bodily injury or property damage claim. For example, a guest of a resident drowns in the pool and that person's parents sue the homeowners association. The homeowners association is found guilty, damages are higher than the limit homeowners association policy, so the excess is passed onto the residents as a loss assessment.

EXCLUSIONS

See page 14 "Things Your Policy Won't Cover"

POLICY CONDITIONS

The conditions section of the homeowners policy details your rights and your insurance company's rights and responsibilities following a loss. The conditions are the same for tenants and unit owners' policies as well except where noted.

Property Coverages

- **Insurable interest** - You can only recover what you lost. If the property is owned by more than one person, each person will only get their share.

- **Duties After Loss** - If you have a loss, you must make sure that you do the following things.

  a. **Prompt notice** - Give your insurance company or agent notice of your loss as soon as possible. The police must be notified if there has been a theft.

  b. **Protect the property** - Take action to be sure that no further damage will occur. For example if a window is broken during a storm, board it up or cover it with a tarp so that no further damage is created.

  c. **Prepare an inventory** - Create a list of damaged property and its value along with pictures and appraisals if necessary. It is helpful to have an inventory before a loss so that creating the list of what was lost will be much easier.

  d. **Show the damaged property** - Do not throw any property away until the insurance company has seen it.

  e. **File a proof of loss** - A proof of loss is a signed sworn document attesting your loss.

- **Loss Settlement** - This section details how a loss will be paid on your policy depending upon the conditions.

- **Loss to a Pair or Set** - The loss of one item in a pair or set doesn't diminish the entire value of the collection. The insurer will pay to replace or repair or pay the difference in the value before and after the loss.

- **Glass Replacement** - The insurer will pay the additional cost to have any broken glass replaced with safety glass or glazing as required by many communities.

- **Appraisal** - This section outlines the procedure for settling disputes between you and your insurer if you don't agree on the amount of the loss.

- **Other Insurance** - If a loss is covered by more than one policy, your insurer will only pay its share of the loss.

- **Suit Against the Insurer** - This section limits the time you have to file suit against your insurance company.

- **Additional Loss Settlement Conditions**

  a. **Insurer's Option** - The insurer can replace items with similar items but not exact duplicates of what was lost.

  b. **Loss Payment** - This defines who will be paid and when the payment will be made.

  c. **Abandonment of Property** - This section prohibits you from leaving your property and saying that it's the insurers responsibility.

  d. **Mortgage Clause** - This section provides that any loss will be paid to the mortgagee if your property is mortgaged.

  e. **No Benefit to Bailee** - No coverage is granted to anyone holding, storing, or moving property for a fee.

  f. **Nuclear Hazard Clause** - Any loss caused by a nuclear hazard will not be considered a loss.

  g. **Recovered Property** - If stolen property is recovered, you must notify the insurer and you must decide to keep the property and return the money or keep the replacement.

  h. **Volcanic Eruption Period** - All volcanic activity in a 72-hour period is considered one occurrence.

Liability Coverages

- **Limit of liability** - The limit shown on the declarations page is the limit of liability for one occurrence regardless of the number of insured's, claims made, or persons injured.

- **Severability of Insurance** - The coverage applies to each insured separately. If a child causes bodily injury to another party, and the child along with his or her parents are sued, the policy will look to see how it applies to each party, and may or may not cover each separately.

- **Duties after loss**

  a. Provide the insured with prompt written notice

  b. Promptly forward to the insurance company any and every legal document you receive regarding the lawsuit

  c. Assist the insurance company in making its settlement and its case by attending hearings and trials

  d. Provide your insurance company a sworn statement about the event.

  e. Do not voluntarily make payment, assume fault, or pay for anything other than first aid at the time of an injury.

- **Duties of an injured person (Medical Payments Coverage)** - You must send written notice to your insurance company as soon as practical. The injured person may then have to send medical records to the insurance company and submit to an exam by a doctor selected by the insurer.

- **Payment of claim (Medical Payments Coverage)** - This section says that just because you pay for first aid costs doesn't mean that you are automatically liable. The injured person cannot automatically collect under the personal liability section of the policy.

- **Suit against the insured** - No legal action against the insurer can be brought unless all of the policy conditions have been met.

- **Bankruptcy of an insured** - Bankruptcy of the insured doesn't relieve the insurer of its obligations under the policy.

- **Other insurance** - If you have other insurance, your homeowners company will only pay its share.

Common Policy Conditions

- **Policy period** - Only losses that occur during the policy period are covered. The policy period is generally one year and is noted on the declarations page.

- **Concealment or fraud** - Coverage is not provided if any information has been concealed before or after a loss. Concealment must be intentional and material for the insurer to void the policy.

- **Liberalization clause** - If the insurance company revises its policies and the revision would broaden your policy without any additional premium, the broadened coverage will apply to your policy automatically.

- **Waiver or change of policy provisions** - Any changes to the policy must be in writing to be valid.

- **Cancellations** - The insured may cancel the policy at any time. The insurer has strict rules about when it can cancel your policy.

- **Nonrenewal** - The insurer may decide not to continue insuring you at your policy renewal, and must notify you 30 days in advance.

- **Assignment** - You cannot give your policy and its coverages to another person without written consent of the insurer.

- **Subrogation** - Subrogation is a way that insurance companies can recoup money that they have already paid to you for a claim. Your insurance company will look to the insurance company of the person who is liable for reimbursement. If the insured has not waived his or her rights to subrogation, the insurer is able to go back to the insurance company of the responsible party for repayment.

- **Death of name insured** - If you or your spouse or other insured listed on your policy dies during the policy term, your legal representative is insured with regard to the property covered under that policy.

Things Your Policy Won't Cover

Although the homeowners policy is considered an all-risk policy and will cover you for any loss you incur, there are some exclusions or causes that it won't cover.

Property Exclusions

Coverage A and B

- **Collapse** - The collapse of your house is excluded unless the cause of loss is listed in the additional coverages section of your policy.

- **Freezing** - Freezing of plumbing, heating, or air conditioning systems is excluded if the heat has not been maintained while the building is vacant, unoccupied, or under construction.

- **Flood** - The most important thing to know is that your policy does NOT cover flood. You must purchase a separate policy to cover damage from a flood. Flood has been an excluded peril since 1968 when the government started the National Flood Insurance Program. Even if you don't live in a designated flood zone, it is important to have flood insurance in the event of hurricanes or heavy rains. Also, premiums for flood insurance can be inexpensive depending upon your flood risk. You can purchase a flood policy through your homeowners insurer or find an agent through the flood program.

  Visit www.FloodSmart.gov to learn how the National Flood Insurance Program defines a flood and learn how much your annual flood insurance premium can cost.

- **Foundations, Retaining Walls, and Nonbuilding Structures** - Loss to these items (including fences, swimming pools, and docks) by freezing, thawing, pressure or weight of water or ice is not covered.

- **Dwelling under Construction** - Theft from a dwelling under construction is excluded. Theft of material is also excluded until the dwelling is finished.

- **Vandalism and Malicious Mischief** - This exclusion only applies if the building has been vacant for more than 30 consecutive days before the loss. (Vacant being empty and unfurnished and unoccupied being a furnished home where the residents are on vacation.)

- **Mold, Fungus or Wet Rot** - Loss caused by Mold, Fungus or Wet Rot is not covered if caused by a sump, sump pump or related equipment or a roof drain, gutter, downspout or similar fixture or equipment. Please review your individual policy carefully in order to comprehend exactly what is covered.

- **Risks of Direct Physical Loss Exclusion** - The homeowners form insures your property against any loss as long as it isn't excluded. This section lists some of the other specific causes that aren't covered. Examples are: wear and tear, smog, birds, rodents, animals owned or kept by an insured, and settling.

- **Concurrent Causation Exclusions** - This section deals with more than one event causing a loss. The policy details how losses are handled when one cause is covered and another isn't.

Coverage A, B, C and D

- **Ordinance or Law** - Loss from the enforcement of any law relating to the construction,repair, or demolition of a building. An endorsement can be added to the policy to add back this coverage.

- **Earth Movement** - This is to exclude damage from earthquakes and landslides. Earthquake coverage can be added back to the policy as an endorsement if you live in an area that may be prone to earthquakes.

- **Water Damage** - This is to exclude flood (which can be purchased separately) as well as sewer backup.

- **Power Failure** - This is to exclude claims for damaged food from power outages.

- **Neglect** - This encourages the insured to take reasonable steps to save endangered property.

- **War** - Damage to your home from war, declared or not is excluded.

Liability Exclusions

Coverage E and F

- **Expected or intended injury or damage** - This section excludes intentional acts.

- **Insured's business** - Any damage or injury that arises out of your business is excluded.

- **Premises rented or held for rental** - There is no coverage for liability arising from renting any part of your property to someone else.

- **Professional services** - This is similar to the business exclusion and excludes liability from providing or not providing professional services.

- **Noninsured locations** - Any location that is not listed on the policy as an insured location.

- **Motor vehicles** - Homeowners policies provide no coverage for liability arising from owning or using a motor or motorized vehicle. Not included in this definition are trailers, golf carts, garden tractor, or motorized wheelchair.

- **Watercraft** - The policy excludes any and all liability arising from owning and using a watercraft.

- **Aircraft** - The policy excludes any and all liability arising from owning and using an aircraft.

- **War** - There is no coverage for liability arising from war.

- **Communicable disease** - There is no liability coverage for infecting another person with a communicable disease.

- **Abuse or sexual molestation** - There is no liability coverage for damage arising out of abuse (physical or mental) or sexual molestation.

- **Controlled substances** - There is no liability coverage for damage arising out of the use, sale, etc. of a controlled substance.

- **Home day care** - Coverage is limited under section 1 (property) but and excluded in section 2 (liability) of the policy. There is usually an endorsement added to the policy that clarifies home day care as a business and thus excludes it. You would need separate coverage to protect yourself against potential liability as a home day care provider.

How Premiums are Determined

Insurance companies take a wide range of factors into consideration when determining how much you will have to pay in premiums. These include:

- **Amount of coverage** - The higher the policy's maximum coverage limits, the higher your premium will be. You may be able to get away with the minimums required by your lender, but go ahead and ask for pricing on replacement value limits before making that decision. Don't forget that you don't need to insure your land, only your home. Depending on the other factors listed below, you may be able to substantially increase your protection for a very modest increase in your premiums.

- **Amount of deductible** - The deductible is the portion of the claim you must pay before the insurance company will pay the remainder. Deductibles typically range from $250 to $2,000. As you might expect, the higher the deductible, the lower your premium will be. Note: if you have wind coverage on your policy for damage from a hurricane, your policy will have a separate and most likely higher deductible specifically for that peril. Usually, this deductible is expressed as a percentage of the insured value of your home. If you have this separate deductible, the percentage as well as the amount should be listed on your declarations page.

- **Location, Location, Location** - Where your house is located will determine how much you will pay. There are many items that are taken into consideration when looking at where your house is located. Warm climate or cold? Urban or rural? Is there a fire department and/or fire hydrant nearby? Is your house oceanfront?

- **Protection** - This primarily pertains to protection from fire and theft. Do you have smoke detectors? Do you have a sprinkler system? How far is the nearest fire hydrant and fire station? Do you have an alarm system? Is it monitored?

- **Construction** - What your house is made of makes a difference as well. Is it wood (frame) construction or is it brick (masonry)? Did the builder use fire-resistive or noncombustible materials?

- **Other items** - Your insurance company will want to know if you have a dog, and what type it is, as well as if you have a pool, and how it is protected. These are items that add some risk, and may increase your premiums. Some insurance companies will not insure people with certain types of dogs.

- **Credit Scores** - Insurance companies have recently started using credit scores as a predictor of future claims activity.

The law does not allow an insurer to use your credit history as the sole factor in determining your premiums. Your credit score can, however, be used against you to decline coverage or as one of several factors used to set your premium. Not all companies use credit scores, so if your credit history is particularly bad, it is all the more important that you shop around for a homeowners policy from an insurer that does not use creditas a factor in setting its premiums. This could easily save you hundreds of dollars per year.

Although these are the basic factors that every insurance company uses in setting its premiums, the amount you pay will still vary from company to company based upon each insurer's underwriting model (the process of assessing your risk and pricing your policy accordingly). Some insurance companies weight some factors more heavily than others. In addition, one company may have had a high level of claims in a particular state, forcing it to raise premiums in that state, whereas another company in the same state may have had a low level of claims there, allowing it to lower premiums in that state.

For these reasons, we strongly encourage you to comparison shop for your homeowners insurance policy. So if you are interested in saving money, it definitely pays to shop around and look at multiple insurers regardless of whether you're buying a new policy or renewing an existing one.

Ways to Save Money on Your Premium

The most effective way to save money on your homeowners insurance premium is to pay smaller claims out of your own pocket and only look to your insurance in the event of a large loss. The fewer claims you have, the more insurers you'll have bidding for your business and the lower their rate quotes will be. Other ways to lower your premium are to:

- **Reduce your risk of theft and fire and ask for discounts if you have any of these items.** Consider installing dead bolts on all outside doors as well as installing a burglar alarm. Also, if you are building or renovating, consider a sprinkler system and the newer higher tech fire resistive materials.

- **Increase your deductible.** Ask your insurer for premium quotes using different deductible levels to see how much you could save by covering a greater portion of the claim cost out of your own pocket. It may be worth it to go with a higher deductible, particularly if you've got the financial capacity to pay a higher deductible in the event of a loss.

Make sure that the damage is significant enough to warrant filing a claim. This is a subjective decision as it will depend on where you have set your deductible. Just make sure you have money set aside in an emergency fund to cover the deductible in the event of a major loss.

- **Compare prices regularly.** Shop your policy around by getting premium quotes from other insurers every year or two. You don't necessarily have to change companies, but this is generally a worthwhile exercise. It's relatively easy to do and you could find another insurer that will save you a significant amount of money on your homeowners insurance.

- **Use the same company for homeowners and auto insurance.** Almost all insurers will give you a discount on your premium if you purchase insurance for both your home and your car from them. Be careful though. Sometimes, even with this discount, you could end up paying more than you would by shopping for the least expensive coverage from two separate, unrelated insurers.

- **Take advantage of group discounts.** If you are a member of a national group like AAA, AARP, AMA, ABA, etc. ask your agent if there are any special discounts for your group. And if you or your parents were in the military, be sure to get a rate quote from USAA, a company that specifically caters to military personnel. As with other discounts, you'll want to make sure that the discounted policy is indeed less expensive than your other alternatives. In other words, don't buy it just because the insurer is giving a discount to your group.

- **Use your clean credit report to your advantage.** Depending upon the laws in your state, insurance companies can use your credit history to grant or deny coverage or as a factor in setting your premium rate. So be sure to get a copy of your credit report and make sure any erroneous information is removed (this is a good idea even when you're not shopping forhomeowners insurance). You'll usually be given the option of whether or not to grant the insurance company access to your credit report. So, if you have decent credit, let them see it and it could save you some money.

- **Pay your premium in advance.** If you can afford it, pay your full annual or semi-annualpolicy premium up front. Some companies actually give you a discount for doing so, while others will charge an extra fee ($3 to $5 each month) if you elect to pay your premiums monthly.

With the growth of the Internet, there is a wealth of additional free information available to help you save money or get better coverage on your homeowners insurance. See the Appendix for a listing of useful websites.

What to do if you have a Claim

- **Should you file the claim or pay it out of pocket?**

  a. Remember, your insurance coverage should be thought of as coverage for a catastrophe or a major loss. The more claims you file, the more expensive your policy will be and you may have an even more difficult time obtaining coverage.

  b. If you do decide to file, you must do it in a timely manner - the sooner the better. Also, you must do whatever you can to protect your property from further damage while waiting for your claim to be handled.

- **Keep good records.**

  a. Even before a claim, you should have records of the major purchases you have made for your home, a listing of items by room, a disc with photos of each room, or a video showing the contents of each room of your home. (The items should be updated every couple of years or when a large purchase is made or remodel is completed.) Also, if possible, take pictures after the loss for further documentation.

  b. Keep receipts for emergency repairs that you make as well as any additional living expenses you incur in the event you are displaced from your home.

  c. Keep copies and notes of any correspondence with your insurance company and its representatives. If you feel that you are not being treated fairly or your claim is not being handled in a timely manner, contact someone higher up at the insurance company. If there is still no resolution, complain to your state's department of insurance. If all else fails, contact an attorney.

  d. Get a quote for repairs from an independent contractor to use in negotiations with your claims adjuster. Get multiple quotes before selecting a contractor.

- **Know your policy**

  a. Read your policy to familiarize yourself with what is and what is not covered, as well as what your deductibles are. Also, read any endorsements that are sent to you with or after your policy is issued. If you know what your policy says, you are better prepared to discuss your claim with your adjuster.

  b. If your adjuster tells you that something is limited or not covered, ask them to show you that language.

How to Shop for a Homeowners Policy

Now that you realize the value of shopping around to get the best rate on your homeowners insurance policy, the next step is to take action. There are three possible routes to go - agents, direct writers, and the Internet - and you should feel free to pursue any or all of them depending on the amount of time and effort you're willing to devote.

Agents

Most people prefer face-to-face interaction and therefore opt to work with an insurance agent. There are pros and cons to this approach, however. On the positive side, a knowledgeable agent can walk you through the entire purchasing process, answering any questions you may have and helping you to select the policy components that are right for you. An agent can also be particularly helpful by assisting you in your dealings with the claims adjuster and the insurance company.

On the downside, not all insurance agents are created equal. Some have lousy customer service, essentially negating the benefits listed above. And others are so focused on increasing their commissions that they try to push you into coverages that you really don't need. Plus, policies available through an agent are generally more expensive than those available through direct writers or the Internet due to the cost of paying the agent's commission.

Finding a good agent is pretty much a hit and miss proposition. Your best bet is to rely on referrals from friends, neighbors, and family members who are happy with their insurance agent. You can also consult your local phone book or do an Internet search to identify more names even though you won't have any information on their quality.

Keep in mind that there are actually two types of insurance agents: exclusive agents that represent only one company and independent agents that represent many companies. If you find an agent who works with only one company, you'll definitely want to check premium prices elsewhere before selecting an insurer to go with. And even if you're working with an independent agent who represents multiple companies, it still doesn't hurt to comparison shop with other agents or on the internet to make sure you're getting the best deal possible.

Bottom line: If your preference is to have someone else do most of the legwork, an agent is your best bet, particularly if he has more than one company to choose from.

Direct Writers

Some insurance companies cut out the middle man (i.e., the agent) and instead employ their own salespeople who perform the agent's functions via phone. These companies are called direct writers. Shopping for a policy from a direct writer can be time consuming since you essentially have to call each company one by one to get a premium quote. At the same time though, some of the best deals can be found through direct writers due to their lower cost structure. You won't get quite the same personalized service as dealing with an agent, but the saving could make the impersonalization worth it to you.

Most direct writers advertise heavily in the mail, on the radio, and on television, so you've probably seen something from at least one of them without realizing you were being solicited by a direct writer. Also, some have started selling their policies through agents and then adding the agent's commission directly onto the premium you pay. Consult the Appendix for a list of websites operated by insurance companies some of which are direct writers.

The Internet

The Internet is a great place to do your comparison shopping. There are a large number of websites that can search through hundreds of insurers to find which ones offer the lowest premiums based on your specific situation. What's more, you can usually get a premium quote immediately after entering some information about yourself.

Some insurance websites require you to give them a great deal of information up front such as your address, your social security number, specific information about your home and its protections, and information about any past claims that you have reported. This can be a lot of work, particularly if you do it for multiple policy searches. Other websites request only basic information in order to give you a ballpark quote. From there, you can decide if it's worth your time to enter all of the details required to get an actual quote.

If you want to get the rock bottom, lowest price possible on your homeowners insurance and you have the time to devote to it, the Internet is probably your best option. You won't have the comfort of consulting with an agent or even dealing with a salesperson. On the other hand, you'll be able to proceed at your own pace, from the comfort of your own home, without anyone pushing you to buy more.

Finding a website that sells homeowners insurance is extremely easy. All you have to do is put "homeowners insurance quotes" into a search engine and you'll get more than you can possibly use. For your convenience, we've also included the web address for some of the major online vendors of homeowners insurance in the Appendix of this publication.

In order to cut down on the time involved with shopping for insurance on the Internet, be sure to supply the most accurate information possible. Your claims history and information about your home will be scrutinized before a policy is issued, so it won't do you any good to try and skirt any blemishes. It will only make the process longer.

When shopping for a homeowners insurance policy, we recommend you follow these steps:

Step 1   Gather all of the personal information that will be needed in order to receive a premium quote. This includes your:

    a. Address
    b. Social security number
    c. Protection information - nearest hydrant, fire station, alarm information
    d. Construction of home including date and materials used
    e. Claims history for past five years whether or not you've lived in the house the entire time
    f. Policy limits and deductibles on your current homeowners policy.

Step 2   Consult with your friends, neighbors, and family members to see who they use for their homeowners insurance and what their level of satisfaction has been.

Step 3   Decide which avenue(s) you'd like to use to shop for your new policy: an agent, a direct writer, or the Internet.

Step 4   Give some consideration to the limits of coverage you are interested in purchasing as well the deductibles. You can always request quotes for multiple options, but it's good to have an idea of what you want going in.

Step 5   Set aside some dedicated, uninterrupted time and contact the agents, companies, or websites you've decided to pursue. A good plan of action will help cut down on the amount of time involved.

Step 6   Take good notes so you can make sure you are getting "apples-to-apples" comparisons and so you will know who to contact if you should select a particular policy. There is a Premium Quote Comparison Worksheet in the Appendix to help you with this process.

Step 7   Narrow your list down to the least expensive two or three quotes and then take a look at those specific companies in more detail. Specifically, check: - Each company's Weiss Safety Rating at www.weissratings.com to make sure the company is financially sound and will be around to pay your claim if you have one. Turn to Weiss recommended homeowners insurers by state for a list. - Contact your state department of insurance to see if they can provide you with any information on the companies' history of consumer complaints or anything else that may aid you in your decision-making process. - Conduct a search on the Internet using the company name. This may turn up postings from others that could be helpful to you.

Step 8   Select a company and submit an application to purchase your policy. If the paperwork comes back with a premium quote that differs from what you were originally quoted, don't hesitate about moving on to your second choice of companies.

Weiss Recommended Homeowners Insurers by State

The following pages list Weiss Recommended Homeowners Insurers (based strictly on financial safety) licensed to do business in each state. These insurers currently receive a Weiss Safety Rating of A+, A, A-, or B+, indicating their strong financial position. Companies are listed by their Safety Rating and then alphabetically within each Safety Rating grouping.If an insurer is not on this list, it should not be automatically assumed that the firm is weak. Indeed, there are many firms that have not achieved a B+ or better rating but are in relatively good condition with adequate resources to cover their risk. Not being included in this list should not be construed as a recommendation to cancel a policy.

To get Weiss Safety Rating for a company not included here, go to www.weissratings.com.

Weiss Safety Rating	Our rating is measured on a scale from A to F and considers a wide range of factors. Highly rated companies are, in our opinion, less likely to experience financial difficulties than lower-rated firms. See "What Our Ratings Mean" in the Appendix for a definition of each rating category.
Name	The insurance company's legally registered name, which can sometimes differ from the name that the company uses for advertising. An insurer's name can be very similar to the name of other companies which may not be on this list, so make sure you note the exact name before contacting your agent.
City, Address, State	The address of the main office where you can contact the firm for additional information or for the location of local branches and/or registered agents.
Telephone	The telephone number to call for information on purchasing an insurance policy from the company.

The following list of recommended Homeowners Insurers by State is based on ratings as of the date of publication.

What Our Ratings Mean

A **Excellent.** The company offers excellent financial security. It has maintained a conservative stance in its investment strategies, business operations and underwriting commitments. While the financial position of any company is subject to change, we believe that this company has the resources necessary to deal with severe economic conditions.

B **Good.** The company offers good financial security and has the resources to deal with a variety of adverse economic conditions. It comfortably exceeds the minimum levels for all of our rating criteria, and is likely to remain healthy for the near future. However, in the event of a severe recession or major financial crisis, we feel that this assessment should be reviewed to make sure that the firm is still maintaining adequate financial strength.

C **Fair.** The company offers fair financial security and is currently stable. But during an economic downturn or other financial pressures, we feel it may encounter difficulties in maintaining its financial stability.

D **Weak.** The company currently demonstrates what, in our opinion, we consider to be significant weaknesses which could negatively impact policyholders. In an unfavorable economic environment, these weaknesses could be magnified.

E **Very Weak.** The company currently demonstrates what we consider to be significant weaknesses and has also failed some of the basic tests that we use to identify fiscal stability. Therefore, even in a favorable economic environment, it is our opinion that policyholders could incur significant risks.

F **Failed.** The company is deemed failed if it is either 1) under supervision of an insurance regulatory authority; 2) in the process of rehabilitation; 3) in the process of liquidation; or 4) voluntarily dissolved after disciplinary or other regulatory action by an insurance regulatory authority.

+ The **plus sign** is an indication that the company is in the upper third of the letter grade.

- The **minus sign** is an indication that the company is in the lower third of the letter grade.

U **Unrated.** The company is unrated for one or more of the following reasons: (1) total assets are less than $1 million; (2) premium income for the current year was less than $100,000; or (3) the company functions almost exclusively as a holding company rather than as an underwriter; or, (4) in our opinion, we do not have enough information to reliably issue a rating.

Alabama

Safety Rating: A

Company	City	Address	State	Zip	Telephone
Cincinnati Ins Co	Fairfield	6200 South Gilmore Road	OH	45014	513-870-2000

Safety Rating: A-

Company	City	Address	State	Zip	Telephone
USAA Casualty Ins Co	San Antonio	9800 Fredericksburg Road	TX	78288	210-498-1411
Owners Ins Co	Lima	2325 North Cole Street	OH	45801	517-323-1200
Country Mutual Ins Co	Bloomington	1701 N Towanda Avenue	IL	61701	309-821-3000
Auto-Owners Ins Co	Lansing	6101 Anacapri Boulevard	MI	48917	517-323-1200

Safety Rating: B+

Company	City	Address	State	Zip	Telephone
USAA General Indemnity Co	San Antonio	9800 Fredericksburg Road	TX	78288	210-498-1411
United Services Automobile Asn	San Antonio	9800 Fredericksburg Road	TX	78288	210-498-2211
State Farm Fire & Cas Co	Bloomington	One State Farm Plaza	IL	61710	309-766-2311
Nationwide Mutual Fire Ins Co	Columbus	One West Nationwide Blvd	OH	43215	614-249-7111
Country Casualty Ins Co	Bloomington	1701 N Towanda Avenue	IL	61701	309-821-3000
Amica Mutual Ins Co	Lincoln	100 Amica Way	RI	02865	800-652-6422
Alfa Mutual General Ins Co	Montgomery	2108 East South Boulevard	AL	36116	334-288-3900

Alaska

Safety Rating: A-

Company	City	Address	State	Zip	Telephone
USAA Casualty Ins Co	San Antonio	9800 Fredericksburg Road	TX	78288	210-498-1411
Country Mutual Ins Co	Bloomington	1701 N Towanda Avenue	IL	61701	309-821-3000

Safety Rating: B+

Company	City	Address	State	Zip	Telephone
USAA General Indemnity Co	San Antonio	9800 Fredericksburg Road	TX	78288	210-498-1411
United Services Automobile Asn	San Antonio	9800 Fredericksburg Road	TX	78288	210-498-2211
State Farm Fire & Cas Co	Bloomington	One State Farm Plaza	IL	61710	309-766-2311

Arizona

Safety Rating: A

Company	City	Address	State	Zip	Telephone
Cincinnati Ins Co	Fairfield	6200 South Gilmore Road	OH	45014	513-870-2000

Safety Rating: A-

Company	City	Address	State	Zip	Telephone
USAA Casualty Ins Co	San Antonio	9800 Fredericksburg Road	TX	78288	210-498-1411

Arizona (continued)

Safety Rating: A-

Company	City	Address	State	Zip	Telephone
Owners Ins Co	Lima	2325 North Cole Street	OH	45801	517-323-1200
Country Mutual Ins Co	Bloomington	1701 N Towanda Avenue	IL	61701	309-821-3000
Auto-Owners Ins Co	Lansing	6101 Anacapri Boulevard	MI	48917	517-323-1200

Safety Rating: B+

Company	City	Address	State	Zip	Telephone
Western Agricultural Ins Co	West Des Moines	5400 University Avenue	IA	50266	515-225-5400
USAA General Indemnity Co	San Antonio	9800 Fredericksburg Road	TX	78288	210-498-1411
United Services Automobile Asn	San Antonio	9800 Fredericksburg Road	TX	78288	210-498-2211
State Farm Fire & Cas Co	Bloomington	One State Farm Plaza	IL	61710	309-766-2311
Pekin Ins Co	Pekin	2505 Court Street	IL	61558	309-346-1161
Nationwide Mutual Fire Ins Co	Columbus	One West Nationwide Blvd	OH	43215	614-249-7111
Farm Bureau P&C Ins Co	West Des Moines	5400 University Avenue	IA	50266	515-225-5400
Amica Mutual Ins Co	Lincoln	100 Amica Way	RI	02865	800-652-6422
American Family Mutl Ins Co SI	Madison	6000 American Parkway	WI	53783	608-249-2111
Acuity A Mutual Ins Co	Sheboygan	2800 South Taylor Drive	WI	53081	920-458-9131

Arkansas

Safety Rating: A

Company	City	Address	State	Zip	Telephone
Cincinnati Ins Co	Fairfield	6200 South Gilmore Road	OH	45014	513-870-2000

Safety Rating: A-

Company	City	Address	State	Zip	Telephone
USAA Casualty Ins Co	San Antonio	9800 Fredericksburg Road	TX	78288	210-498-1411
Auto-Owners Ins Co	Lansing	6101 Anacapri Boulevard	MI	48917	517-323-1200

Safety Rating: B+

Company	City	Address	State	Zip	Telephone
USAA General Indemnity Co	San Antonio	9800 Fredericksburg Road	TX	78288	210-498-1411
United Services Automobile Asn	San Antonio	9800 Fredericksburg Road	TX	78288	210-498-2211
State Farm Fire & Cas Co	Bloomington	One State Farm Plaza	IL	61710	309-766-2311
Nationwide Mutual Fire Ins Co	Columbus	One West Nationwide Blvd	OH	43215	614-249-7111
Amica Mutual Ins Co	Lincoln	100 Amica Way	RI	02865	800-652-6422

California

Safety Rating: A

Company	City	Address	State	Zip	Telephone
Tokio Marine America Ins Co	New York	230 Park Avenue	NY	10169	610-227-1253

California (continued)

Safety Rating: A

Company	City	Address	State	Zip	Telephone
Cincinnati Ins Co	Fairfield	6200 South Gilmore Road	OH	45014	513-870-2000

Safety Rating: A-

Company	City	Address	State	Zip	Telephone
USAA Casualty Ins Co	San Antonio	9800 Fredericksburg Road	TX	78288	210-498-1411

Safety Rating: B+

Company	City	Address	State	Zip	Telephone
USAA General Indemnity Co	San Antonio	9800 Fredericksburg Road	TX	78288	210-498-1411
United Services Automobile Asn	San Antonio	9800 Fredericksburg Road	TX	78288	210-498-2211
Nationwide Mutual Fire Ins Co	Columbus	One West Nationwide Blvd	OH	43215	614-249-7111
Interins Exchange	Costa Mesa	3333 Fairview Road	CA	92626	714-850-5111
Amica Mutual Ins Co	Lincoln	100 Amica Way	RI	02865	800-652-6422

Colorado

Safety Rating: A

Company	City	Address	State	Zip	Telephone
Cincinnati Ins Co	Fairfield	6200 South Gilmore Road	OH	45014	513-870-2000

Safety Rating: A-

Company	City	Address	State	Zip	Telephone
USAA Casualty Ins Co	San Antonio	9800 Fredericksburg Road	TX	78288	210-498-1411
Owners Ins Co	Lima	2325 North Cole Street	OH	45801	517-323-1200
Country Mutual Ins Co	Bloomington	1701 N Towanda Avenue	IL	61701	309-821-3000
Auto-Owners Ins Co	Lansing	6101 Anacapri Boulevard	MI	48917	517-323-1200

Safety Rating: B+

Company	City	Address	State	Zip	Telephone
USAA General Indemnity Co	San Antonio	9800 Fredericksburg Road	TX	78288	210-498-1411
United Services Automobile Asn	San Antonio	9800 Fredericksburg Road	TX	78288	210-498-2211
State Farm Fire & Cas Co	Bloomington	One State Farm Plaza	IL	61710	309-766-2311
National Casualty Co	Scottsdale	8877 N Gainey Center Drive	AZ	85258	480-365-4000
Amica Mutual Ins Co	Lincoln	100 Amica Way	RI	02865	800-652-6422
American Family Mutl Ins Co SI	Madison	6000 American Parkway	WI	53783	608-249-2111
Acuity A Mutual Ins Co	Sheboygan	2800 South Taylor Drive	WI	53081	920-458-9131

Connecticut

Safety Rating: A

Company	City	Address	State	Zip	Telephone
Cincinnati Ins Co	Fairfield	6200 South Gilmore Road	OH	45014	513-870-2000

Safety Rating: A-

Company	City	Address	State	Zip	Telephone
USAA Casualty Ins Co	San Antonio	9800 Fredericksburg Road	TX	78288	210-498-1411

Safety Rating: B+

Company	City	Address	State	Zip	Telephone
USAA General Indemnity Co	San Antonio	9800 Fredericksburg Road	TX	78288	210-498-1411
United Services Automobile Asn	San Antonio	9800 Fredericksburg Road	TX	78288	210-498-2211
State Farm Fire & Cas Co	Bloomington	One State Farm Plaza	IL	61710	309-766-2311
Nationwide Mutual Fire Ins Co	Columbus	One West Nationwide Blvd	OH	43215	614-249-7111
Farm Family Casualty Ins Co	Glenmont	344 Route 9w	NY	12077	518-431-5000
Amica Mutual Ins Co	Lincoln	100 Amica Way	RI	02865	800-652-6422

Delaware

Safety Rating: A-

Company	City	Address	State	Zip	Telephone
USAA Casualty Ins Co	San Antonio	9800 Fredericksburg Road	TX	78288	210-498-1411

Safety Rating: B+

Company	City	Address	State	Zip	Telephone
USAA General Indemnity Co	San Antonio	9800 Fredericksburg Road	TX	78288	210-498-1411
United Services Automobile Asn	San Antonio	9800 Fredericksburg Road	TX	78288	210-498-2211
State Farm Fire & Cas Co	Bloomington	One State Farm Plaza	IL	61710	309-766-2311
Nationwide Mutual Fire Ins Co	Columbus	One West Nationwide Blvd	OH	43215	614-249-7111
Farm Family Casualty Ins Co	Glenmont	344 Route 9w	NY	12077	518-431-5000
Amica Mutual Ins Co	Lincoln	100 Amica Way	RI	02865	800-652-6422

District of Columbia

Safety Rating: A

Company	City	Address	State	Zip	Telephone
Cincinnati Ins Co	Fairfield	6200 South Gilmore Road	OH	45014	513-870-2000

Safety Rating: A-

Company	City	Address	State	Zip	Telephone
USAA Casualty Ins Co	San Antonio	9800 Fredericksburg Road	TX	78288	210-498-1411

District of Columbia (continued)

Safety Rating: B+

Company	City	Address	State	Zip	Telephone
USAA General Indemnity Co	San Antonio	9800 Fredericksburg Road	TX	78288	210-498-1411
United Services Automobile Asn	San Antonio	9800 Fredericksburg Road	TX	78288	210-498-2211
State Farm Fire & Cas Co	Bloomington	One State Farm Plaza	IL	61710	309-766-2311
Nationwide Mutual Fire Ins Co	Columbus	One West Nationwide Blvd	OH	43215	614-249-7111
Amica Mutual Ins Co	Lincoln	100 Amica Way	RI	02865	800-652-6422

Florida

Safety Rating: A+

Company	City	Address	State	Zip	Telephone
Citizens Property Ins Corp	Tallahassee	2312 Killearn Ctr Blvd Bldg A	FL	32303	850-513-3700

Safety Rating: A

Company	City	Address	State	Zip	Telephone
Cincinnati Ins Co	Fairfield	6200 South Gilmore Road	OH	45014	513-870-2000

Safety Rating: A-

Company	City	Address	State	Zip	Telephone
USAA Casualty Ins Co	San Antonio	9800 Fredericksburg Road	TX	78288	210-498-1411
Southern-Owners Ins Co	Lansing	6101 Anacapri Boulevard	MI	48917	517-323-1200

Safety Rating: B+

Company	City	Address	State	Zip	Telephone
USAA General Indemnity Co	San Antonio	9800 Fredericksburg Road	TX	78288	210-498-1411
United Services Automobile Asn	San Antonio	9800 Fredericksburg Road	TX	78288	210-498-2211
Amica Mutual Ins Co	Lincoln	100 Amica Way	RI	02865	800-652-6422

Georgia

Safety Rating: A

Company	City	Address	State	Zip	Telephone
Cincinnati Ins Co	Fairfield	6200 South Gilmore Road	OH	45014	513-870-2000

Safety Rating: A-

Company	City	Address	State	Zip	Telephone
USAA Casualty Ins Co	San Antonio	9800 Fredericksburg Road	TX	78288	210-498-1411
Travelers Casualty & Surety Co	Hartford	One Tower Square	CT	06183	860-277-0111
Owners Ins Co	Lima	2325 North Cole Street	OH	45801	517-323-1200
Country Mutual Ins Co	Bloomington	1701 N Towanda Avenue	IL	61701	309-821-3000
Auto-Owners Ins Co	Lansing	6101 Anacapri Boulevard	MI	48917	517-323-1200

Georgia (continued)

Safety Rating: B+

Company	City	Address	State	Zip	Telephone
USAA General Indemnity Co	San Antonio	9800 Fredericksburg Road	TX	78288	210-498-1411
United Services Automobile Asn	San Antonio	9800 Fredericksburg Road	TX	78288	210-498-2211
Travelers Indemnity Co	Hartford	One Tower Square	CT	06183	860-277-0111
State Farm Fire & Cas Co	Bloomington	One State Farm Plaza	IL	61710	309-766-2311
Nationwide Mutual Fire Ins Co	Columbus	One West Nationwide Blvd	OH	43215	614-249-7111
Country Casualty Ins Co	Bloomington	1701 N Towanda Avenue	IL	61701	309-821-3000
Amica Mutual Ins Co	Lincoln	100 Amica Way	RI	02865	800-652-6422

Hawaii

Safety Rating: A-

Company	City	Address	State	Zip	Telephone
USAA Casualty Ins Co	San Antonio	9800 Fredericksburg Road	TX	78288	210-498-1411

Safety Rating: B+

Company	City	Address	State	Zip	Telephone
USAA General Indemnity Co	San Antonio	9800 Fredericksburg Road	TX	78288	210-498-1411
United Services Automobile Asn	San Antonio	9800 Fredericksburg Road	TX	78288	210-498-2211
Travelers Indemnity Co	Hartford	One Tower Square	CT	06183	860-277-0111
State Farm Fire & Cas Co	Bloomington	One State Farm Plaza	IL	61710	309-766-2311
Interins Exchange	Costa Mesa	3333 Fairview Road	CA	92626	714-850-5111

Idaho

Safety Rating: A

Company	City	Address	State	Zip	Telephone
Cincinnati Ins Co	Fairfield	6200 South Gilmore Road	OH	45014	513-870-2000

Safety Rating: A-

Company	City	Address	State	Zip	Telephone
USAA Casualty Ins Co	San Antonio	9800 Fredericksburg Road	TX	78288	210-498-1411
Country Mutual Ins Co	Bloomington	1701 N Towanda Avenue	IL	61701	309-821-3000
Auto-Owners Ins Co	Lansing	6101 Anacapri Boulevard	MI	48917	517-323-1200

Safety Rating: B+

Company	City	Address	State	Zip	Telephone
USAA General Indemnity Co	San Antonio	9800 Fredericksburg Road	TX	78288	210-498-1411
United Services Automobile Asn	San Antonio	9800 Fredericksburg Road	TX	78288	210-498-2211
State Farm Fire & Cas Co	Bloomington	One State Farm Plaza	IL	61710	309-766-2311
Amica Mutual Ins Co	Lincoln	100 Amica Way	RI	02865	800-652-6422
American Family Mutl Ins Co SI	Madison	6000 American Parkway	WI	53783	608-249-2111

Idaho (continued)

Safety Rating: B+

Company	City	Address	State	Zip	Telephone
Acuity A Mutual Ins Co	Sheboygan	2800 South Taylor Drive	WI	53081	920-458-9131

Illinois

Safety Rating: A

Company	City	Address	State	Zip	Telephone
Cincinnati Ins Co	Fairfield	6200 South Gilmore Road	OH	45014	513-870-2000

Safety Rating: A-

Company	City	Address	State	Zip	Telephone
USAA Casualty Ins Co	San Antonio	9800 Fredericksburg Road	TX	78288	210-498-1411
Travelers Casualty & Surety Co	Hartford	One Tower Square	CT	06183	860-277-0111
Owners Ins Co	Lima	2325 North Cole Street	OH	45801	517-323-1200
Country Mutual Ins Co	Bloomington	1701 N Towanda Avenue	IL	61701	309-821-3000
Auto-Owners Ins Co	Lansing	6101 Anacapri Boulevard	MI	48917	517-323-1200

Safety Rating: B+

Company	City	Address	State	Zip	Telephone
West Bend Mutual Ins Co	West Bend	1900 South 18th Avenue	WI	53095	262-334-5571
USAA General Indemnity Co	San Antonio	9800 Fredericksburg Road	TX	78288	210-498-1411
United Services Automobile Asn	San Antonio	9800 Fredericksburg Road	TX	78288	210-498-2211
State Farm Fire & Cas Co	Bloomington	One State Farm Plaza	IL	61710	309-766-2311
Pekin Ins Co	Pekin	2505 Court Street	IL	61558	309-346-1161
Nationwide Mutual Fire Ins Co	Columbus	One West Nationwide Blvd	OH	43215	614-249-7111
Farmers Automobile Ins Asn	Pekin	2505 Court Street	IL	61558	309-346-1161
Country Casualty Ins Co	Bloomington	1701 N Towanda Avenue	IL	61701	309-821-3000
Amica Mutual Ins Co	Lincoln	100 Amica Way	RI	02865	800-652-6422
American Family Mutl Ins Co SI	Madison	6000 American Parkway	WI	53783	608-249-2111
Acuity A Mutual Ins Co	Sheboygan	2800 South Taylor Drive	WI	53081	920-458-9131

Indiana

Safety Rating: A

Company	City	Address	State	Zip	Telephone
Cincinnati Ins Co	Fairfield	6200 South Gilmore Road	OH	45014	513-870-2000

Safety Rating: A-

Company	City	Address	State	Zip	Telephone
USAA Casualty Ins Co	San Antonio	9800 Fredericksburg Road	TX	78288	210-498-1411
Owners Ins Co	Lima	2325 North Cole Street	OH	45801	517-323-1200
Country Mutual Ins Co	Bloomington	1701 N Towanda Avenue	IL	61701	309-821-3000

Indiana (continued)

Safety Rating: A-

Company	City	Address	State	Zip	Telephone
Auto-Owners Ins Co	Lansing	6101 Anacapri Boulevard	MI	48917	517-323-1200

Safety Rating: B+

Company	City	Address	State	Zip	Telephone
West Bend Mutual Ins Co	West Bend	1900 South 18th Avenue	WI	53095	262-334-5571
USAA General Indemnity Co	San Antonio	9800 Fredericksburg Road	TX	78288	210-498-1411
United Services Automobile Asn	San Antonio	9800 Fredericksburg Road	TX	78288	210-498-2211
State Farm Fire & Cas Co	Bloomington	One State Farm Plaza	IL	61710	309-766-2311
Property-Owners Ins Co	Marion	3950 West Delphi Pike	IN	46952	517-323-1200
Pekin Ins Co	Pekin	2505 Court Street	IL	61558	309-346-1161
Nationwide Mutual Fire Ins Co	Columbus	One West Nationwide Blvd	OH	43215	614-249-7111
Motorists Mutual Ins Co	Columbus	471 East Broad Street	OH	43215	614-225-8211
Farmers Automobile Ins Asn	Pekin	2505 Court Street	IL	61558	309-346-1161
Amica Mutual Ins Co	Lincoln	100 Amica Way	RI	02865	800-652-6422
American Family Mutl Ins Co SI	Madison	6000 American Parkway	WI	53783	608-249-2111
Acuity A Mutual Ins Co	Sheboygan	2800 South Taylor Drive	WI	53081	920-458-9131

Iowa

Safety Rating: A

Company	City	Address	State	Zip	Telephone
Cincinnati Ins Co	Fairfield	6200 South Gilmore Road	OH	45014	513-870-2000

Safety Rating: A-

Company	City	Address	State	Zip	Telephone
USAA Casualty Ins Co	San Antonio	9800 Fredericksburg Road	TX	78288	210-498-1411
Owners Ins Co	Lima	2325 North Cole Street	OH	45801	517-323-1200
Country Mutual Ins Co	Bloomington	1701 N Towanda Avenue	IL	61701	309-821-3000
Auto-Owners Ins Co	Lansing	6101 Anacapri Boulevard	MI	48917	517-323-1200

Safety Rating: B+

Company	City	Address	State	Zip	Telephone
Western Agricultural Ins Co	West Des Moines	5400 University Avenue	IA	50266	515-225-5400
West Bend Mutual Ins Co	West Bend	1900 South 18th Avenue	WI	53095	262-334-5571
USAA General Indemnity Co	San Antonio	9800 Fredericksburg Road	TX	78288	210-498-1411
United Services Automobile Asn	San Antonio	9800 Fredericksburg Road	TX	78288	210-498-2211
State Farm Fire & Cas Co	Bloomington	One State Farm Plaza	IL	61710	309-766-2311
Pekin Ins Co	Pekin	2505 Court Street	IL	61558	309-346-1161
Farmers Automobile Ins Asn	Pekin	2505 Court Street	IL	61558	309-346-1161
Farm Bureau P&C Ins Co	West Des Moines	5400 University Avenue	IA	50266	515-225-5400
Amica Mutual Ins Co	Lincoln	100 Amica Way	RI	02865	800-652-6422

Iowa (continued)

Safety Rating: B+

Company	City	Address	State	Zip	Telephone
American Family Mutl Ins Co SI	Madison	6000 American Parkway	WI	53783	608-249-2111
Acuity A Mutual Ins Co	Sheboygan	2800 South Taylor Drive	WI	53081	920-458-9131

Kansas

Safety Rating: A

Company	City	Address	State	Zip	Telephone
Cincinnati Ins Co	Fairfield	6200 South Gilmore Road	OH	45014	513-870-2000

Safety Rating: A-

Company	City	Address	State	Zip	Telephone
USAA Casualty Ins Co	San Antonio	9800 Fredericksburg Road	TX	78288	210-498-1411
Country Mutual Ins Co	Bloomington	1701 N Towanda Avenue	IL	61701	309-821-3000
Auto-Owners Ins Co	Lansing	6101 Anacapri Boulevard	MI	48917	517-323-1200

Safety Rating: B+

Company	City	Address	State	Zip	Telephone
Western Agricultural Ins Co	West Des Moines	5400 University Avenue	IA	50266	515-225-5400
USAA General Indemnity Co	San Antonio	9800 Fredericksburg Road	TX	78288	210-498-1411
United Services Automobile Asn	San Antonio	9800 Fredericksburg Road	TX	78288	210-498-2211
Travelers Indemnity Co	Hartford	One Tower Square	CT	06183	860-277-0111
State Farm Fire & Cas Co	Bloomington	One State Farm Plaza	IL	61710	309-766-2311
Farm Bureau P&C Ins Co	West Des Moines	5400 University Avenue	IA	50266	515-225-5400
Country Casualty Ins Co	Bloomington	1701 N Towanda Avenue	IL	61701	309-821-3000
Amica Mutual Ins Co	Lincoln	100 Amica Way	RI	02865	800-652-6422
American Family Mutl Ins Co SI	Madison	6000 American Parkway	WI	53783	608-249-2111
Acuity A Mutual Ins Co	Sheboygan	2800 South Taylor Drive	WI	53081	920-458-9131

Kentucky

Safety Rating: A

Company	City	Address	State	Zip	Telephone
Cincinnati Ins Co	Fairfield	6200 South Gilmore Road	OH	45014	513-870-2000

Safety Rating: A-

Company	City	Address	State	Zip	Telephone
USAA Casualty Ins Co	San Antonio	9800 Fredericksburg Road	TX	78288	210-498-1411
Owners Ins Co	Lima	2325 North Cole Street	OH	45801	517-323-1200
Auto-Owners Ins Co	Lansing	6101 Anacapri Boulevard	MI	48917	517-323-1200

Kentucky (continued)

Safety Rating: B+

Company	City	Address	State	Zip	Telephone
USAA General Indemnity Co	San Antonio	9800 Fredericksburg Road	TX	78288	210-498-1411
United Services Automobile Asn	San Antonio	9800 Fredericksburg Road	TX	78288	210-498-2211
State Farm Fire & Cas Co	Bloomington	One State Farm Plaza	IL	61710	309-766-2311
Nationwide Mutual Fire Ins Co	Columbus	One West Nationwide Blvd	OH	43215	614-249-7111
National Casualty Co	Scottsdale	8877 N Gainey Center Drive	AZ	85258	480-365-4000
Motorists Mutual Ins Co	Columbus	471 East Broad Street	OH	43215	614-225-8211
Amica Mutual Ins Co	Lincoln	100 Amica Way	RI	02865	800-652-6422

Louisiana

Safety Rating: A-

Company	City	Address	State	Zip	Telephone
USAA Casualty Ins Co	San Antonio	9800 Fredericksburg Road	TX	78288	210-498-1411

Safety Rating: B+

Company	City	Address	State	Zip	Telephone
USAA General Indemnity Co	San Antonio	9800 Fredericksburg Road	TX	78288	210-498-1411
United Services Automobile Asn	San Antonio	9800 Fredericksburg Road	TX	78288	210-498-2211
State Farm Fire & Cas Co	Bloomington	One State Farm Plaza	IL	61710	309-766-2311
Amica Mutual Ins Co	Lincoln	100 Amica Way	RI	02865	800-652-6422

Maine

Safety Rating: A

Company	City	Address	State	Zip	Telephone
Cincinnati Ins Co	Fairfield	6200 South Gilmore Road	OH	45014	513-870-2000

Safety Rating: A-

Company	City	Address	State	Zip	Telephone
USAA Casualty Ins Co	San Antonio	9800 Fredericksburg Road	TX	78288	210-498-1411

Safety Rating: B+

Company	City	Address	State	Zip	Telephone
USAA General Indemnity Co	San Antonio	9800 Fredericksburg Road	TX	78288	210-498-1411
United Services Automobile Asn	San Antonio	9800 Fredericksburg Road	TX	78288	210-498-2211
State Farm Fire & Cas Co	Bloomington	One State Farm Plaza	IL	61710	309-766-2311
Nationwide Mutual Fire Ins Co	Columbus	One West Nationwide Blvd	OH	43215	614-249-7111
Interins Exchange	Costa Mesa	3333 Fairview Road	CA	92626	714-850-5111
Farm Family Casualty Ins Co	Glenmont	344 Route 9w	NY	12077	518-431-5000
Amica Mutual Ins Co	Lincoln	100 Amica Way	RI	02865	800-652-6422
Acuity A Mutual Ins Co	Sheboygan	2800 South Taylor Drive	WI	53081	920-458-9131

Maryland

Safety Rating: A

Company	City	Address	State	Zip	Telephone
Cincinnati Ins Co	Fairfield	6200 South Gilmore Road	OH	45014	513-870-2000

Safety Rating: A-

Company	City	Address	State	Zip	Telephone
USAA Casualty Ins Co	San Antonio	9800 Fredericksburg Road	TX	78288	210-498-1411

Safety Rating: B+

Company	City	Address	State	Zip	Telephone
USAA General Indemnity Co	San Antonio	9800 Fredericksburg Road	TX	78288	210-498-1411
United Services Automobile Asn	San Antonio	9800 Fredericksburg Road	TX	78288	210-498-2211
State Farm Fire & Cas Co	Bloomington	One State Farm Plaza	IL	61710	309-766-2311
Nationwide Mutual Fire Ins Co	Columbus	One West Nationwide Blvd	OH	43215	614-249-7111
Amica Mutual Ins Co	Lincoln	100 Amica Way	RI	02865	800-652-6422

Massachusetts

Safety Rating: A

Company	City	Address	State	Zip	Telephone
Sentry Ins A Mutual Co	Stevens Point	1800 North Point Drive	WI	54481	715-346-6000
Cincinnati Ins Co	Fairfield	6200 South Gilmore Road	OH	45014	513-870-2000

Safety Rating: A-

Company	City	Address	State	Zip	Telephone
USAA Casualty Ins Co	San Antonio	9800 Fredericksburg Road	TX	78288	210-498-1411
Motorists Commercial Mutual Ins Co	Columbus	471 East Broad Street	OH	43215	614-225-8211

Safety Rating: B+

Company	City	Address	State	Zip	Telephone
USAA General Indemnity Co	San Antonio	9800 Fredericksburg Road	TX	78288	210-498-1411
United Services Automobile Asn	San Antonio	9800 Fredericksburg Road	TX	78288	210-498-2211
Travelers Indemnity Co	Hartford	One Tower Square	CT	06183	860-277-0111
State Farm Fire & Cas Co	Bloomington	One State Farm Plaza	IL	61710	309-766-2311
National Casualty Co	Scottsdale	8877 N Gainey Center Drive	AZ	85258	480-365-4000
Farm Family Casualty Ins Co	Glenmont	344 Route 9w	NY	12077	518-431-5000
Amica Mutual Ins Co	Lincoln	100 Amica Way	RI	02865	800-652-6422

Michigan

Safety Rating: A

Company	City	Address	State	Zip	Telephone
Cincinnati Ins Co	Fairfield	6200 South Gilmore Road	OH	45014	513-870-2000

Michigan (continued)

Safety Rating: A-

Company	City	Address	State	Zip	Telephone
USAA Casualty Ins Co	San Antonio	9800 Fredericksburg Road	TX	78288	210-498-1411
Home-Owners Ins Co	Lansing	6101 Anacapri Boulevard	MI	48917	517-323-1200
Auto-Owners Ins Co	Lansing	6101 Anacapri Boulevard	MI	48917	517-323-1200

Safety Rating: B+

Company	City	Address	State	Zip	Telephone
United Services Automobile Asn	San Antonio	9800 Fredericksburg Road	TX	78288	210-498-2211
State Farm Fire & Cas Co	Bloomington	One State Farm Plaza	IL	61710	309-766-2311
Nationwide Mutual Fire Ins Co	Columbus	One West Nationwide Blvd	OH	43215	614-249-7111
Amica Mutual Ins Co	Lincoln	100 Amica Way	RI	02865	800-652-6422

Minnesota

Safety Rating: A

Company	City	Address	State	Zip	Telephone
Cincinnati Ins Co	Fairfield	6200 South Gilmore Road	OH	45014	513-870-2000

Safety Rating: A-

Company	City	Address	State	Zip	Telephone
USAA Casualty Ins Co	San Antonio	9800 Fredericksburg Road	TX	78288	210-498-1411
Owners Ins Co	Lima	2325 North Cole Street	OH	45801	517-323-1200
Country Mutual Ins Co	Bloomington	1701 N Towanda Avenue	IL	61701	309-821-3000
Auto-Owners Ins Co	Lansing	6101 Anacapri Boulevard	MI	48917	517-323-1200

Safety Rating: B+

Company	City	Address	State	Zip	Telephone
Western Agricultural Ins Co	West Des Moines	5400 University Avenue	IA	50266	515-225-5400
West Bend Mutual Ins Co	West Bend	1900 South 18th Avenue	WI	53095	262-334-5571
USAA General Indemnity Co	San Antonio	9800 Fredericksburg Road	TX	78288	210-498-1411
United Services Automobile Asn	San Antonio	9800 Fredericksburg Road	TX	78288	210-498-2211
State Farm Fire & Cas Co	Bloomington	One State Farm Plaza	IL	61710	309-766-2311
Farm Bureau P&C Ins Co	West Des Moines	5400 University Avenue	IA	50266	515-225-5400
Amica Mutual Ins Co	Lincoln	100 Amica Way	RI	02865	800-652-6422
American Family Mutl Ins Co SI	Madison	6000 American Parkway	WI	53783	608-249-2111
Acuity A Mutual Ins Co	Sheboygan	2800 South Taylor Drive	WI	53081	920-458-9131

Mississippi

Safety Rating: A

Company	City	Address	State	Zip	Telephone
Cincinnati Ins Co	Fairfield	6200 South Gilmore Road	OH	45014	513-870-2000

39

Mississippi (continued)

Safety Rating: A-

Company	City	Address	State	Zip	Telephone
USAA Casualty Ins Co	San Antonio	9800 Fredericksburg Road	TX	78288	210-498-1411

Safety Rating: B+

Company	City	Address	State	Zip	Telephone
USAA General Indemnity Co	San Antonio	9800 Fredericksburg Road	TX	78288	210-498-1411
United Services Automobile Asn	San Antonio	9800 Fredericksburg Road	TX	78288	210-498-2211
State Farm Fire & Cas Co	Bloomington	One State Farm Plaza	IL	61710	309-766-2311
Nationwide Mutual Fire Ins Co	Columbus	One West Nationwide Blvd	OH	43215	614-249-7111
Amica Mutual Ihs Co	Lincoln	100 Amica Way	RI	02865	800-652-6422

Missouri

Safety Rating: A

Company	City	Address	State	Zip	Telephone
Cincinnati Ins Co	Fairfield	6200 South Gilmore Road	OH	45014	513-870-2000

Safety Rating: A-

Company	City	Address	State	Zip	Telephone
USAA Casualty Ins Co	San Antonio	9800 Fredericksburg Road	TX	78288	210-498-1411
Country Mutual Ins Co	Bloomington	1701 N Towanda Avenue	IL	61701	309-821-3000
Auto-Owners Ins Co	Lansing	6101 Anacapri Boulevard	MI	48917	517-323-1200

Safety Rating: B+

Company	City	Address	State	Zip	Telephone
USAA General Indemnity Co	San Antonio	9800 Fredericksburg Road	TX	78288	210-498-1411
United Services Automobile Asn	San Antonio	9800 Fredericksburg Road	TX	78288	210-498-2211
State Farm Fire & Cas Co	Bloomington	One State Farm Plaza	IL	61710	309-766-2311
Amica Mutual Ins Co	Lincoln	100 Amica Way	RI	02865	800-652-6422
American Family Mutl Ins Co SI	Madison	6000 American Parkway	WI	53783	608-249-2111
Acuity A Mutual Ins Co	Sheboygan	2800 South Taylor Drive	WI	53081	920-458-9131

Montana

Safety Rating: A

Company	City	Address	State	Zip	Telephone
Cincinnati Ins Co	Fairfield	6200 South Gilmore Road	OH	45014	513-870-2000

Safety Rating: A-

Company	City	Address	State	Zip	Telephone
USAA Casualty Ins Co	San Antonio	9800 Fredericksburg Road	TX	78288	210-498-1411

Montana (continued)

Safety Rating: B+

Company	City	Address	State	Zip	Telephone
USAA General Indemnity Co	San Antonio	9800 Fredericksburg Road	TX	78288	210-498-1411
United Services Automobile Asn	San Antonio	9800 Fredericksburg Road	TX	78288	210-498-2211
State Farm Fire & Cas Co	Bloomington	One State Farm Plaza	IL	61710	309-766-2311
Amica Mutual Ins Co	Lincoln	100 Amica Way	RI	02865	800-652-6422
Acuity A Mutual Ins Co	Sheboygan	2800 South Taylor Drive	WI	53081	920-458-9131

Nebraska

Safety Rating: A

Company	City	Address	State	Zip	Telephone
Cincinnati Ins Co	Fairfield	6200 South Gilmore Road	OH	45014	513-870-2000

Safety Rating: A-

Company	City	Address	State	Zip	Telephone
USAA Casualty Ins Co	San Antonio	9800 Fredericksburg Road	TX	78288	210-498-1411
Auto-Owners Ins Co	Lansing	6101 Anacapri Boulevard	MI	48917	517-323-1200

Safety Rating: B+

Company	City	Address	State	Zip	Telephone
Western Agricultural Ins Co	West Des Moines	5400 University Avenue	IA	50266	515-225-5400
USAA General Indemnity Co	San Antonio	9800 Fredericksburg Road	TX	78288	210-498-1411
United Services Automobile Asn	San Antonio	9800 Fredericksburg Road	TX	78288	210-498-2211
State Farm Fire & Cas Co	Bloomington	One State Farm Plaza	IL	61710	309-766-2311
Farm Bureau P&C Ins Co	West Des Moines	5400 University Avenue	IA	50266	515-225-5400
Amica Mutual Ins Co	Lincoln	100 Amica Way	RI	02865	800-652-6422
American Family Mutl Ins Co SI	Madison	6000 American Parkway	WI	53783	608-249-2111

Nevada

Safety Rating: A

Company	City	Address	State	Zip	Telephone
Cincinnati Ins Co	Fairfield	6200 South Gilmore Road	OH	45014	513-870-2000

Safety Rating: A-

Company	City	Address	State	Zip	Telephone
USAA Casualty Ins Co	San Antonio	9800 Fredericksburg Road	TX	78288	210-498-1411
Country Mutual Ins Co	Bloomington	1701 N Towanda Avenue	IL	61701	309-821-3000

Safety Rating: B+

Company	City	Address	State	Zip	Telephone
USAA General Indemnity Co	San Antonio	9800 Fredericksburg Road	TX	78288	210-498-1411

Nevada (continued)

Safety Rating: B+

Company	City	Address	State	Zip	Telephone
United Services Automobile Asn	San Antonio	9800 Fredericksburg Road	TX	78288	210-498-2211
State Farm Fire & Cas Co	Bloomington	One State Farm Plaza	IL	61710	309-766-2311
National Casualty Co	Scottsdale	8877 N Gainey Center Drive	AZ	85258	480-365-4000
Amica Mutual Ins Co	Lincoln	100 Amica Way	RI	02865	800-652-6422
American Family Mutl Ins Co SI	Madison	6000 American Parkway	WI	53783	608-249-2111
Acuity A Mutual Ins Co	Sheboygan	2800 South Taylor Drive	WI	53081	920-458-9131

New Hampshire

Safety Rating: A

Company	City	Address	State	Zip	Telephone
Cincinnati Ins Co	Fairfield	6200 South Gilmore Road	OH	45014	513-870-2000

Safety Rating: A-

Company	City	Address	State	Zip	Telephone
USAA Casualty Ins Co	San Antonio	9800 Fredericksburg Road	TX	78288	210-498-1411

Safety Rating: B+

Company	City	Address	State	Zip	Telephone
USAA General Indemnity Co	San Antonio	9800 Fredericksburg Road	TX	78288	210-498-1411
United Services Automobile Asn	San Antonio	9800 Fredericksburg Road	TX	78288	210-498-2211
State Farm Fire & Cas Co	Bloomington	One State Farm Plaza	IL	61710	309-766-2311
Nationwide Mutual Fire Ins Co	Columbus	One West Nationwide Blvd	OH	43215	614-249-7111
Interins Exchange	Costa Mesa	3333 Fairview Road	CA	92626	714-850-5111
Farm Family Casualty Ins Co	Glenmont	344 Route 9w	NY	12077	518-431-5000
Amica Mutual Ins Co	Lincoln	100 Amica Way	RI	02865	800-652-6422

New Jersey

Safety Rating: A

Company	City	Address	State	Zip	Telephone
Cincinnati Ins Co	Fairfield	6200 South Gilmore Road	OH	45014	513-870-2000

Safety Rating: A-

Company	City	Address	State	Zip	Telephone
USAA Casualty Ins Co	San Antonio	9800 Fredericksburg Road	TX	78288	210-498-1411

Safety Rating: B+

Company	City	Address	State	Zip	Telephone
USAA General Indemnity Co	San Antonio	9800 Fredericksburg Road	TX	78288	210-498-1411
United Services Automobile Asn	San Antonio	9800 Fredericksburg Road	TX	78288	210-498-2211

New Jersey (continued)

Safety Rating: B+

Company	City	Address	State	Zip	Telephone
State Farm Fire & Cas Co	Bloomington	One State Farm Plaza	IL	61710	309-766-2311
Amica Mutual Ins Co	Lincoln	100 Amica Way	RI	02865	800-652-6422
Allstate NJ Ins Co	Northbrook	2775 Sanders Road	IL	60062	908-252-5000

New Mexico

Safety Rating: A

Company	City	Address	State	Zip	Telephone
Cincinnati Ins Co	Fairfield	6200 South Gilmore Road	OH	45014	513-870-2000

Safety Rating: A-

Company	City	Address	State	Zip	Telephone
USAA Casualty Ins Co	San Antonio	9800 Fredericksburg Road	TX	78288	210-498-1411

Safety Rating: B+

Company	City	Address	State	Zip	Telephone
Western Agricultural Ins Co	West Des Moines	5400 University Avenue	IA	50266	515-225-5400
USAA General Indemnity Co	San Antonio	9800 Fredericksburg Road	TX	78288	210-498-1411
United Services Automobile Asn	San Antonio	9800 Fredericksburg Road	TX	78288	210-498-2211
State Farm Fire & Cas Co	Bloomington	One State Farm Plaza	IL	61710	309-766-2311
Interins Exchange	Costa Mesa	3333 Fairview Road	CA	92626	714-850-5111
Farm Bureau P&C Ins Co	West Des Moines	5400 University Avenue	IA	50266	515-225-5400
Amica Mutual Ins Co	Lincoln	100 Amica Way	RI	02865	800-652-6422
Acuity A Mutual Ins Co	Sheboygan	2800 South Taylor Drive	WI	53081	920-458-9131

New York

Safety Rating: A

Company	City	Address	State	Zip	Telephone
Cincinnati Ins Co	Fairfield	6200 South Gilmore Road	OH	45014	513-870-2000

Safety Rating: A-

Company	City	Address	State	Zip	Telephone
USAA Casualty Ins Co	San Antonio	9800 Fredericksburg Road	TX	78288	210-498-1411
Travelers Casualty & Surety Co	Hartford	One Tower Square	CT	06183	860-277-0111

Safety Rating: B+

Company	City	Address	State	Zip	Telephone
USAA General Indemnity Co	San Antonio	9800 Fredericksburg Road	TX	78288	210-498-1411
United Services Automobile Asn	San Antonio	9800 Fredericksburg Road	TX	78288	210-498-2211
State Farm Fire & Cas Co	Bloomington	One State Farm Plaza	IL	61710	309-766-2311

New York (continued)

Safety Rating: B+

Company	City	Address	State	Zip	Telephone
Nationwide Mutual Fire Ins Co	Columbus	One West Nationwide Blvd	OH	43215	614-249-7111
Farm Family Casualty Ins Co	Glenmont	344 Route 9w	NY	12077	518-431-5000
Amica Mutual Ins Co	Lincoln	100 Amica Way	RI	02865	800-652-6422

North Carolina

Safety Rating: A

Company	City	Address	State	Zip	Telephone
Cincinnati Ins Co	Fairfield	6200 South Gilmore Road	OH	45014	513-870-2000

Safety Rating: A-

Company	City	Address	State	Zip	Telephone
USAA Casualty Ins Co	San Antonio	9800 Fredericksburg Road	TX	78288	210-498-1411
Travelers Casualty & Surety Co	Hartford	One Tower Square	CT	06183	860-277-0111
Owners Ins Co	Lima	2325 North Cole Street	OH	45801	517-323-1200
Auto-Owners Ins Co	Lansing	6101 Anacapri Boulevard	MI	48917	517-323-1200

Safety Rating: B+

Company	City	Address	State	Zip	Telephone
USAA General Indemnity Co	San Antonio	9800 Fredericksburg Road	TX	78288	210-498-1411
United Services Automobile Asn	San Antonio	9800 Fredericksburg Road	TX	78288	210-498-2211
Travelers Indemnity Co	Hartford	One Tower Square	CT	06183	860-277-0111
State Farm Fire & Cas Co	Bloomington	One State Farm Plaza	IL	61710	309-766-2311
Nationwide Mutual Fire Ins Co	Columbus	One West Nationwide Blvd	OH	43215	614-249-7111
Amica Mutual Ins Co	Lincoln	100 Amica Way	RI	02865	800-652-6422

North Dakota

Safety Rating: A

Company	City	Address	State	Zip	Telephone
Cincinnati Ins Co	Fairfield	6200 South Gilmore Road	OH	45014	513-870-2000

Safety Rating: A-

Company	City	Address	State	Zip	Telephone
USAA Casualty Ins Co	San Antonio	9800 Fredericksburg Road	TX	78288	210-498-1411
Owners Ins Co	Lima	2325 North Cole Street	OH	45801	517-323-1200
Country Mutual Ins Co	Bloomington	1701 N Towanda Avenue	IL	61701	309-821-3000
Auto-Owners Ins Co	Lansing	6101 Anacapri Boulevard	MI	48917	517-323-1200

North Dakota (continued)

Safety Rating: B+

Company	City	Address	State	Zip	Telephone
USAA General Indemnity Co	San Antonio	9800 Fredericksburg Road	TX	78288	210-498-1411
United Services Automobile Asn	San Antonio	9800 Fredericksburg Road	TX	78288	210-498-2211
State Farm Fire & Cas Co	Bloomington	One State Farm Plaza	IL	61710	309-766-2311
Country Casualty Ins Co	Bloomington	1701 N Towanda Avenue	IL	61701	309-821-3000
Amica Mutual Ins Co	Lincoln	100 Amica Way	RI	02865	800-652-6422
American Family Mutl Ins Co SI	Madison	6000 American Parkway	WI	53783	608-249-2111
Acuity A Mutual Ins Co	Sheboygan	2800 South Taylor Drive	WI	53081	920-458-9131

Ohio

Safety Rating: A

Company	City	Address	State	Zip	Telephone
Cincinnati Ins Co	Fairfield	6200 South Gilmore Road	OH	45014	513-870-2000

Safety Rating: A-

Company	City	Address	State	Zip	Telephone
USAA Casualty Ins Co	San Antonio	9800 Fredericksburg Road	TX	78288	210-498-1411
Owners Ins Co	Lima	2325 North Cole Street	OH	45801	517-323-1200
Home-Owners Ins Co	Lansing	6101 Anacapri Boulevard	MI	48917	517-323-1200
Auto-Owners Ins Co	Lansing	6101 Anacapri Boulevard	MI	48917	517-323-1200

Safety Rating: B+

Company	City	Address	State	Zip	Telephone
USAA General Indemnity Co	San Antonio	9800 Fredericksburg Road	TX	78288	210-498-1411
United Services Automobile Asn	San Antonio	9800 Fredericksburg Road	TX	78288	210-498-2211
State Farm Fire & Cas Co	Bloomington	One State Farm Plaza	IL	61710	309-766-2311
Pekin Ins Co	Pekin	2505 Court Street	IL	61558	309-346-1161
Nationwide Mutual Fire Ins Co	Columbus	One West Nationwide Blvd	OH	43215	614-249-7111
Motorists Mutual Ins Co	Columbus	471 East Broad Street	OH	43215	614-225-8211
Amica Mutual Ins Co	Lincoln	100 Amica Way	RI	02865	800-652-6422
American Family Mutl Ins Co SI	Madison	6000 American Parkway	WI	53783	608-249-2111
Acuity A Mutual Ins Co	Sheboygan	2800 South Taylor Drive	WI	53081	920-458-9131

Oklahoma

Safety Rating: A-

Company	City	Address	State	Zip	Telephone
USAA Casualty Ins Co	San Antonio	9800 Fredericksburg Road	TX	78288	210-498-1411
Country Mutual Ins Co	Bloomington	1701 N Towanda Avenue	IL	61701	309-821-3000

Oklahoma (continued)

Safety Rating: B+

Company	City	Address	State	Zip	Telephone
USAA General Indemnity Co	San Antonio	9800 Fredericksburg Road	TX	78288	210-498-1411
United Services Automobile Asn	San Antonio	9800 Fredericksburg Road	TX	78288	210-498-2211
State Farm Fire & Cas Co	Bloomington	One State Farm Plaza	IL	61710	309-766-2311
Nationwide Mutual Fire Ins Co	Columbus	One West Nationwide Blvd	OH	43215	614-249-7111
Amica Mutual Ins Co	Lincoln	100 Amica Way	RI	02865	800-652-6422

Oregon

Safety Rating: A

Company	City	Address	State	Zip	Telephone
Cincinnati Ins Co	Fairfield	6200 South Gilmore Road	OH	45014	513-870-2000

Safety Rating: A-

Company	City	Address	State	Zip	Telephone
USAA Casualty Ins Co	San Antonio	9800 Fredericksburg Road	TX	78288	210-498-1411
Country Mutual Ins Co	Bloomington	1701 N Towanda Avenue	IL	61701	309-821-3000

Safety Rating: B+

Company	City	Address	State	Zip	Telephone
USAA General Indemnity Co	San Antonio	9800 Fredericksburg Road	TX	78288	210-498-1411
United Services Automobile Asn	San Antonio	9800 Fredericksburg Road	TX	78288	210-498-2211
State Farm Fire & Cas Co	Bloomington	One State Farm Plaza	IL	61710	309-766-2311
Nationwide Mutual Fire Ins Co	Columbus	One West Nationwide Blvd	OH	43215	614-249-7111
Country Casualty Ins Co	Bloomington	1701 N Towanda Avenue	IL	61701	309-821-3000
Amica Mutual Ins Co	Lincoln	100 Amica Way	RI	02865	800-652-6422
American Family Mutl Ins Co SI	Madison	6000 American Parkway	WI	53783	608-249-2111

Pennsylvania

Safety Rating: A

Company	City	Address	State	Zip	Telephone
Cincinnati Ins Co	Fairfield	6200 South Gilmore Road	OH	45014	513-870-2000

Safety Rating: A-

Company	City	Address	State	Zip	Telephone
USAA Casualty Ins Co	San Antonio	9800 Fredericksburg Road	TX	78288	210-498-1411
Auto-Owners Ins Co	Lansing	6101 Anacapri Boulevard	MI	48917	517-323-1200

Safety Rating: B+

Company	City	Address	State	Zip	Telephone
USAA General Indemnity Co	San Antonio	9800 Fredericksburg Road	TX	78288	210-498-1411

Pennsylvania (continued)

Safety Rating: B+

Company	City	Address	State	Zip	Telephone
United Services Automobile Asn	San Antonio	9800 Fredericksburg Road	TX	78288	210-498-2211
Travelers Indemnity Co	Hartford	One Tower Square	CT	06183	860-277-0111
State Farm Fire & Cas Co	Bloomington	One State Farm Plaza	IL	61710	309-766-2311
Nationwide Mutual Fire Ins Co	Columbus	One West Nationwide Blvd	OH	43215	614-249-7111
Motorists Mutual Ins Co	Columbus	471 East Broad Street	OH	43215	614-225-8211
Interins Exchange	Costa Mesa	3333 Fairview Road	CA	92626	714-850-5111
Amica Mutual Ins Co	Lincoln	100 Amica Way	RI	02865	800-652-6422
Acuity A Mutual Ins Co	Sheboygan	2800 South Taylor Drive	WI	53081	920-458-9131

Rhode Island

Safety Rating: A

Company	City	Address	State	Zip	Telephone
Cincinnati Ins Co	Fairfield	6200 South Gilmore Road	OH	45014	513-870-2000

Safety Rating: A-

Company	City	Address	State	Zip	Telephone
USAA Casualty Ins Co	San Antonio	9800 Fredericksburg Road	TX	78288	210-498-1411

Safety Rating: B+

Company	City	Address	State	Zip	Telephone
USAA General Indemnity Co	San Antonio	9800 Fredericksburg Road	TX	78288	210-498-1411
United Services Automobile Asn	San Antonio	9800 Fredericksburg Road	TX	78288	210-498-2211
State Farm Fire & Cas Co	Bloomington	One State Farm Plaza	IL	61710	309-766-2311
Nationwide Mutual Fire Ins Co	Columbus	One West Nationwide Blvd	OH	43215	614-249-7111
Farm Family Casualty Ins Co	Glenmont	344 Route 9w	NY	12077	518-431-5000
Amica Mutual Ins Co	Lincoln	100 Amica Way	RI	02865	800-652-6422

South Carolina

Safety Rating: A

Company	City	Address	State	Zip	Telephone
Cincinnati Ins Co	Fairfield	6200 South Gilmore Road	OH	45014	513-870-2000

Safety Rating: A-

Company	City	Address	State	Zip	Telephone
USAA Casualty Ins Co	San Antonio	9800 Fredericksburg Road	TX	78288	210-498-1411
Owners Ins Co	Lima	2325 North Cole Street	OH	45801	517-323-1200
Auto-Owners Ins Co	Lansing	6101 Anacapri Boulevard	MI	48917	517-323-1200

South Carolina (continued)

Safety Rating: B+

Company	City	Address	State	Zip	Telephone
USAA General Indemnity Co	San Antonio	9800 Fredericksburg Road	TX	78288	210-498-1411
United Services Automobile Asn	San Antonio	9800 Fredericksburg Road	TX	78288	210-498-2211
State Farm Fire & Cas Co	Bloomington	One State Farm Plaza	IL	61710	309-766-2311
Nationwide Mutual Fire Ins Co	Columbus	One West Nationwide Blvd	OH	43215	614-249-7111
Amica Mutual Ins Co	Lincoln	100 Amica Way	RI	02865	800-652-6422

South Dakota

Safety Rating: A

Company	City	Address	State	Zip	Telephone
Cincinnati Ins Co	Fairfield	6200 South Gilmore Road	OH	45014	513-870-2000

Safety Rating: A-

Company	City	Address	State	Zip	Telephone
USAA Casualty Ins Co	San Antonio	9800 Fredericksburg Road	TX	78288	210-498-1411
Auto-Owners Ins Co	Lansing	6101 Anacapri Boulevard	MI	48917	517-323-1200

Safety Rating: B+

Company	City	Address	State	Zip	Telephone
Western Agricultural Ins Co	West Des Moines	5400 University Avenue	IA	50266	515-225-5400
USAA General Indemnity Co	San Antonio	9800 Fredericksburg Road	TX	78288	210-498-1411
United Services Automobile Asn	San Antonio	9800 Fredericksburg Road	TX	78288	210-498-2211
State Farm Fire & Cas Co	Bloomington	One State Farm Plaza	IL	61710	309-766-2311
Farm Bureau P&C Ins Co	West Des Moines	5400 University Avenue	IA	50266	515-225-5400
Amica Mutual Ins Co	Lincoln	100 Amica Way	RI	02865	800-652-6422
American Family Mutl Ins Co SI	Madison	6000 American Parkway	WI	53783	608-249-2111
Acuity A Mutual Ins Co	Sheboygan	2800 South Taylor Drive	WI	53081	920-458-9131

Tennessee

Safety Rating: A

Company	City	Address	State	Zip	Telephone
Cincinnati Ins Co	Fairfield	6200 South Gilmore Road	OH	45014	513-870-2000

Safety Rating: A-

Company	City	Address	State	Zip	Telephone
USAA Casualty Ins Co	San Antonio	9800 Fredericksburg Road	TX	78288	210-498-1411
Country Mutual Ins Co	Bloomington	1701 N Towanda Avenue	IL	61701	309-821-3000
Auto-Owners Ins Co	Lansing	6101 Anacapri Boulevard	MI	48917	517-323-1200

Tennessee (continued)

Safety Rating: B+

Company	City	Address	State	Zip	Telephone
USAA General Indemnity Co	San Antonio	9800 Fredericksburg Road	TX	78288	210-498-1411
United Services Automobile Asn	San Antonio	9800 Fredericksburg Road	TX	78288	210-498-2211
Tennessee Farmers Mutual Ins Co	Columbia	147 Bear Creek Pike	TN	38401	931-388-7872
State Farm Fire & Cas Co	Bloomington	One State Farm Plaza	IL	61710	309-766-2311
Nationwide Mutual Fire Ins Co	Columbus	One West Nationwide Blvd	OH	43215	614-249-7111
National Casualty Co	Scottsdale	8877 N Gainey Center Drive	AZ	85258	480-365-4000
Country Casualty Ins Co	Bloomington	1701 N Towanda Avenue	IL	61701	309-821-3000
Amica Mutual Ins Co	Lincoln	100 Amica Way	RI	02865	800-652-6422
Acuity A Mutual Ins Co	Sheboygan	2800 South Taylor Drive	WI	53081	920-458-9131

Texas

Safety Rating: A-

Company	City	Address	State	Zip	Telephone
USAA Casualty Ins Co	San Antonio	9800 Fredericksburg Road	TX	78288	210-498-1411

Safety Rating: B+

Company	City	Address	State	Zip	Telephone
USAA General Indemnity Co	San Antonio	9800 Fredericksburg Road	TX	78288	210-498-1411
United Services Automobile Asn	San Antonio	9800 Fredericksburg Road	TX	78288	210-498-2211
Interins Exchange	Costa Mesa	3333 Fairview Road	CA	92626	714-850-5111
Auto Club Indemnity Co	Coppell	1225 Freeport Parkway	TX	75019	714-850-5111
Amica Mutual Ins Co	Lincoln	100 Amica Way	RI	02865	800-652-6422

Utah

Safety Rating: A

Company	City	Address	State	Zip	Telephone
Cincinnati Ins Co	Fairfield	6200 South Gilmore Road	OH	45014	513-870-2000

Safety Rating: A-

Company	City	Address	State	Zip	Telephone
USAA Casualty Ins Co	San Antonio	9800 Fredericksburg Road	TX	78288	210-498-1411
Owners Ins Co	Lima	2325 North Cole Street	OH	45801	517-323-1200
Auto-Owners Ins Co	Lansing	6101 Anacapri Boulevard	MI	48917	517-323-1200

Safety Rating: B+

Company	City	Address	State	Zip	Telephone
Western Agricultural Ins Co	West Des Moines	5400 University Avenue	IA	50266	515-225-5400
USAA General Indemnity Co	San Antonio	9800 Fredericksburg Road	TX	78288	210-498-1411
United Services Automobile Asn	San Antonio	9800 Fredericksburg Road	TX	78288	210-498-2211

Utah (continued)

Safety Rating: B+

Company	City	Address	State	Zip	Telephone
State Farm Fire & Cas Co	Bloomington	One State Farm Plaza	IL	61710	309-766-2311
National Casualty Co	Scottsdale	8877 N Gainey Center Drive	AZ	85258	480-365-4000
Farm Bureau P&C Ins Co	West Des Moines	5400 University Avenue	IA	50266	515-225-5400
Amica Mutual Ins Co	Lincoln	100 Amica Way	RI	02865	800-652-6422
American Family Mutl Ins Co SI	Madison	6000 American Parkway	WI	53783	608-249-2111
Acuity A Mutual Ins Co	Sheboygan	2800 South Taylor Drive	WI	53081	920-458-9131

Vermont

Safety Rating: A

Company	City	Address	State	Zip	Telephone
Cincinnati Ins Co	Fairfield	6200 South Gilmore Road	OH	45014	513-870-2000

Safety Rating: A-

Company	City	Address	State	Zip	Telephone
USAA Casualty Ins Co	San Antonio	9800 Fredericksburg Road	TX	78288	210-498-1411

Safety Rating: B+

Company	City	Address	State	Zip	Telephone
USAA General Indemnity Co	San Antonio	9800 Fredericksburg Road	TX	78288	210-498-1411
United Services Automobile Asn	San Antonio	9800 Fredericksburg Road	TX	78288	210-498-2211
State Farm Fire & Cas Co	Bloomington	One State Farm Plaza	IL	61710	309-766-2311
Nationwide Mutual Fire Ins Co	Columbus	One West Nationwide Blvd	OH	43215	614-249-7111
Interins Exchange	Costa Mesa	3333 Fairview Road	CA	92626	714-850-5111
Farm Family Casualty Ins Co	Glenmont	344 Route 9w	NY	12077	518-431-5000
Amica Mutual Ins Co	Lincoln	100 Amica Way	RI	02865	800-652-6422
Acuity A Mutual Ins Co	Sheboygan	2800 South Taylor Drive	WI	53081	920-458-9131

Virginia

Safety Rating: A

Company	City	Address	State	Zip	Telephone
Cincinnati Ins Co	Fairfield	6200 South Gilmore Road	OH	45014	513-870-2000

Safety Rating: A-

Company	City	Address	State	Zip	Telephone
USAA Casualty Ins Co	San Antonio	9800 Fredericksburg Road	TX	78288	210-498-1411
Travelers Casualty & Surety Co	Hartford	One Tower Square	CT	06183	860-277-0111
Owners Ins Co	Lima	2325 North Cole Street	OH	45801	517-323-1200
Auto-Owners Ins Co	Lansing	6101 Anacapri Boulevard	MI	48917	517-323-1200

Virginia (continued)

Safety Rating: B+

Company	City	Address	State	Zip	Telephone
USAA General Indemnity Co	San Antonio	9800 Fredericksburg Road	TX	78288	210-498-1411
United Services Automobile Asn	San Antonio	9800 Fredericksburg Road	TX	78288	210-498-2211
State Farm Fire & Cas Co	Bloomington	One State Farm Plaza	IL	61710	309-766-2311
Nationwide Mutual Fire Ins Co	Columbus	One West Nationwide Blvd	OH	43215	614-249-7111
Interins Exchange	Costa Mesa	3333 Fairview Road	CA	92626	714-850-5111
Amica Mutual Ins Co	Lincoln	100 Amica Way	RI	02865	800-652-6422

Washington

Safety Rating: A-

Company	City	Address	State	Zip	Telephone
USAA Casualty Ins Co	San Antonio	9800 Fredericksburg Road	TX	78288	210-498-1411
Country Mutual Ins Co	Bloomington	1701 N Towanda Avenue	IL	61701	309-821-3000

Safety Rating: B+

Company	City	Address	State	Zip	Telephone
USAA General Indemnity Co	San Antonio	9800 Fredericksburg Road	TX	78288	210-498-1411
United Services Automobile Asn	San Antonio	9800 Fredericksburg Road	TX	78288	210-498-2211
State Farm Fire & Cas Co	Bloomington	One State Farm Plaza	IL	61710	309-766-2311
Nationwide Mutual Fire Ins Co	Columbus	One West Nationwide Blvd	OH	43215	614-249-7111
Country Casualty Ins Co	Bloomington	1701 N Towanda Avenue	IL	61701	309-821-3000
Amica Mutual Ins Co	Lincoln	100 Amica Way	RI	02865	800-652-6422
American Family Mutl Ins Co SI	Madison	6000 American Parkway	WI	53783	608-249-2111

West Virginia

Safety Rating: A

Company	City	Address	State	Zip	Telephone
Cincinnati Ins Co	Fairfield	6200 South Gilmore Road	OH	45014	513-870-2000

Safety Rating: A-

Company	City	Address	State	Zip	Telephone
USAA Casualty Ins Co	San Antonio	9800 Fredericksburg Road	TX	78288	210-498-1411

Safety Rating: B+

Company	City	Address	State	Zip	Telephone
USAA General Indemnity Co	San Antonio	9800 Fredericksburg Road	TX	78288	210-498-1411
United Services Automobile Asn	San Antonio	9800 Fredericksburg Road	TX	78288	210-498-2211
State Farm Fire & Cas Co	Bloomington	One State Farm Plaza	IL	61710	309-766-2311
Nationwide Mutual Fire Ins Co	Columbus	One West Nationwide Blvd	OH	43215	614-249-7111
Motorists Mutual Ins Co	Columbus	471 East Broad Street	OH	43215	614-225-8211

West Virginia (continued)

Safety Rating: B+

Company	City	Address	State	Zip	Telephone
Amica Mutual Ins Co	Lincoln	100 Amica Way	RI	02865	800-652-6422

Wisconsin

Safety Rating: A

Company	City	Address	State	Zip	Telephone
Cincinnati Ins Co	Fairfield	6200 South Gilmore Road	OH	45014	513-870-2000

Safety Rating: A-

Company	City	Address	State	Zip	Telephone
USAA Casualty Ins Co	San Antonio	9800 Fredericksburg Road	TX	78288	210-498-1411
Travelers Casualty & Surety Co	Hartford	One Tower Square	CT	06183	860-277-0111
Owners Ins Co	Lima	2325 North Cole Street	OH	45801	517-323-1200
Country Mutual Ins Co	Bloomington	1701 N Towanda Avenue	IL	61701	309-821-3000
Auto-Owners Ins Co	Lansing	6101 Anacapri Boulevard	MI	48917	517-323-1200

Safety Rating: B+

Company	City	Address	State	Zip	Telephone
West Bend Mutual Ins Co	West Bend	1900 South 18th Avenue	WI	53095	262-334-5571
USAA General Indemnity Co	San Antonio	9800 Fredericksburg Road	TX	78288	210-498-1411
United Services Automobile Asn	San Antonio	9800 Fredericksburg Road	TX	78288	210-498-2211
State Farm Fire & Cas Co	Bloomington	One State Farm Plaza	IL	61710	309-766-2311
Pekin Ins Co	Pekin	2505 Court Street	IL	61558	309-346-1161
Farmers Automobile Ins Asn	Pekin	2505 Court Street	IL	61558	309-346-1161
Amica Mutual Ins Co	Lincoln	100 Amica Way	RI	02865	800-652-6422
American Family Mutl Ins Co SI	Madison	6000 American Parkway	WI	53783	608-249-2111
Acuity A Mutual Ins Co	Sheboygan	2800 South Taylor Drive	WI	53081	920-458-9131

Wyoming

Safety Rating: A

Company	City	Address	State	Zip	Telephone
Cincinnati Ins Co	Fairfield	6200 South Gilmore Road	OH	45014	513-870-2000

Safety Rating: A-

Company	City	Address	State	Zip	Telephone
USAA Casualty Ins Co	San Antonio	9800 Fredericksburg Road	TX	78288	210-498-1411

Safety Rating: B+

Company	City	Address	State	Zip	Telephone
USAA General Indemnity Co	San Antonio	9800 Fredericksburg Road	TX	78288	210-498-1411

Wyoming (continued)

Safety Rating: B+

Company	City	Address	State	Zip	Telephone
United Services Automobile Asn	San Antonio	9800 Fredericksburg Road	TX	78288	210-498-2211
State Farm Fire & Cas Co	Bloomington	One State Farm Plaza	IL	61710	309-766-2311
National Casualty Co	Scottsdale	8877 N Gainey Center Drive	AZ	85258	480-365-4000
Amica Mutual Ins Co	Lincoln	100 Amica Way	RI	02865	800-652-6422
Acuity A Mutual Ins Co	Sheboygan	2800 South Taylor Drive	WI	53081	920-458-9131

Appendix

Quote Comparison Worksheet

Using the worksheet below is a great way to stay organized as you compare the premium quotes from different insurance companies. It allows you to easily compare companies and how much they will charge you for each type of coverage you may be considering.

If you are planning to contact more than three companies, be sure to make copies of this worksheet beforehand.

Company Name						
Phone # or Web Address						
	Limit/Deductible	Price	Limit/Deductible	Price	Limit/Deductible	Price
Coverage A - Dwelling						
Coverage B - Other Structures						
Coverage C - Personal Property						
Coverage D - Loss of Use						
Additional Coverage						
Coverage E						
Coverage F						
Endorsements						
Other						
Discounts						
TOTAL						

Helpful Resources

Contact any of the following organizations for further information about purchasing homeowners insurance.

Your state department of insurance - See next page for a specific contact

National Association of Insurance Commissioners - www.naic.org

Insurance Information Institute - www.iii.org

Independent Insurance Agents & Brokers of America - www.independentagent.com/default.aspx

Weiss Ratings, LLC. - www.weissratings.com

The following is a partial listing of websites that give homeowners insurance quotes. Weiss Ratings does not endorse any of these companies, nor do we warranty any of the information you may obtain from these sites. This information is being provided strictly for your reference only to show the vast number of sites available when shopping for homeowners insurance.

Company websites

www.Allstate.com

www.Amica.com

www.BankersInsurance.com

www.ElectricInsurance.com

www.Geico.com

www.LibertyMutual.com

www.Nationwide.com

www.StateFarm.com

www.thehartford.com/aarp

www.Travelers.com

www.UniversalProperty.com

www.USAA.com

Independent websites

www.AllQuotesInsurance.com

www.homeinsurance.org

www.HomeownersWiz.com

www.Insure.com

www.insureme.com

www.NetQuote.com

State Insurance Commissioners' Departmental Contact Information

State	Official's Title	Website Address	Phone Number
Alabama	Commissioner	www.aldoi.org	(334) 241-4141
Alaska	Director	www.commerce.state.ak.us/insurance/	(800) 467-8725
Arizona	Director	www.id.state.az.us	(800) 325-2548
Arkansas	Commissioner	www.insurance.arkansas.gov	(800) 282-9134
California	Commissioner	www.insurance.ca.gov	(800) 927-4357
Colorado	Commissioner	www.dora.state.co.us/insurance/	(800) 866-7675
Connecticut	Commissioner	www.ct.gov/cid/	(800) 203-3447
Delaware	Commissioner	http://delawareinsurance.gov/	(800) 282-8611
Dist. of Columbia	Commissioner	disr.dc.gov/disr/	(202) 727-8000
Florida	Commissioner	www.floir.com/	(850) 413-3140
Georgia	Commissioner	www.oci.ga.gov/	(800) 656-2298
Hawaii	Commissioner	http://hawaii.gov/dcca/ins/	(808) 586-2790
Idaho	Director	www.doi.idaho.gov	(800) 721-3272
Illinois	Director	www.insurance.illinois.gov/td>	(877) 527-9431
Indiana	Commissioner	www.in.gov/idoi/	(317) 232-2385
Iowa	Commissioner	www.iid.state.ia.us	(877) 955-1212
Kansas	Commissioner	www.ksinsurance.org	(800) 432-2484
Kentucky	Executive Director	http://insurance.ky.gov/	(800) 595-6053
Louisiana	Commissioner	www.ldi.la.gov/	(800) 259-5300
Maine	Superintendent	www.maine.gov/pfr/insurance/	(800) 300-5000
Maryland	Commissioner	www.mdinsurance.state.md.us	(877) 634-6361
Massachusetts	Commissioner	www.mass.gov/ocabr/government/oca-agencies/doi-lp/	(877) 563-4467
Michigan	Commissioner	www.michigan.gov/cis/	(877) 999-6442
Minnesota	Commissioner	http://mn.gov/commerce/insurance/	(651) 296-4026
Mississippi	Commissioner	www.mid.state.ms.us/	(800) 562-2957
Missouri	Director	www.insurance.mo.gov	(800) 726-7390
Montana	Commissioner	www.csi.mt.gov/	(800) 332-6148
Nebraska	Director	www.doi.ne.gov/	(877) 564-7323
Nevada	Commissioner	www.doi.nv.gov/	(888) 872-3234
New Hampshire	Commissioner	www.nh.gov/insurance/	(800) 852-3416
New Jersey	Commissioner	www.state.nj.us/dobi/	(800) 446-7467
New Mexico	Superintendent	www.nmprc.state.nm.us/insurance/	(888) 427-5772
New York	Superintendent	www.dfs.ny.gov/insurance/dfs_insurance.htm	(800) 342-3736
North Carolina	Commissioner	www.ncdoi.com	(800) 546-5664
North Dakota	Commissioner	www.nd.gov/ndins/	(800) 247-0560
Ohio	Director	www.insurance.ohio.gov	(800) 686-1526
Oklahoma	Commissioner	www.ok.gov/oid/	(800) 522-0071
Oregon	Insurance Administrator	www.cbs.state.or.us/ins/	(888) 877-4894
Pennsylvania	Commissioner	www.insurance.pa.gov	(877) 881-6388
Puerto Rico	Commissioner	www.ocs.gobierno.pr	(787) 304-8686
Rhode Island	Superintendent	www.dbr.state.ri.us/divisions/insurance/	(401) 462-9500
South Carolina	Director	www.doi.sc.gov	(800) 768-3467
South Dakota	Director	http://dlr.sd.gov/insurance/default.aspx	(605) 773-3563
Tennessee	Commissioner	www.state.tn.us/commerce/insurance/	(800) 342-4029
Texas	Commissioner	www.tdi.texas.gov/	(800) 252-3439
Utah	Commissioner	www.insurance.utah.gov	(800) 439-3805
Vermont	Commissioner	www.dfr.vermont.gov/insurance/home	(802) 828-3301
Virgin Islands	Lieutenant Governor	www.ltg.gov.vi	(340) 774-7166
Virginia	Commissioner	www.scc.virginia.gov/boi/index.aspx	(800) 552-7945
Washington	Commissioner	www.insurance.wa.gov	(800) 562-6900
West Virginia	Commissioner	www.wvinsurance.gov	(888) 879-9842
Wisconsin	Commissioner	oci.wi.gov	(800) 236-8517
Wyoming	Commissioner	insurance.state.wy.us	(800) 438-5768

Glossary

This glossary contains the most important terms used in this publication.

Actual Cash Value   Insurance that provides the replacement value of property minus depreciation. Unless your policy specifies otherwise, this is the standard coverage.

Additional Living Expense   An increase in your living costs after a covered loss that prevents you from living in your own home. This may include paying for a hotel, restaurant meals, or laundromat, for example.

Agent   An insurance professional that sells insurance for one or more insurance companies. Exclusive agents sell for one company while independent agents sell for more than one company.

All-Risk Coverage   All-risk coverage includes any cause of loss that is not specifically excluded from the policy. Also known as special form coverage.

Basic Form or Basic Causes of Loss   The basic causes of loss consist of the following: fire, lightning, windstorm, hail, explosion, riot or civil commotion, aircraft, vehicles, smoke, vandalism or malicious mischief, theft, and volcanic eruption.

Broad Form or Broad Causes of Loss   The broad causes of loss consist of the basic causes of loss plus the following: falling objects; weight of ice, sleet, or snow; damage by broken window glass; accidental discharge from a plumbing or heating system; sudden and accidental tearing apart, cracking, burning, or bulging of a steam or hot water system; and freezing of plumbing or of a heating or air conditioning system.

Claim   A request to your insurance company to pay for your loss or damage you caused that is covered under your insurance policy. First-party claims are your claims to your company, and third-party claims are your claims against another person's insurance company.

Coverage A - Dwelling	The part of your policy that covers the house itself.
Coverage B - Other Structures	The part of your policy that covers any other buildings such as barns, sheds, and garages, on your property. The amount of coverage is usually 10% of Coverage A.
Coverage C - Personal Property	The part of your policy that covers your belongings including furniture. The amount of coverage is usually 50% of Coverage A.
Coverage D - Loss of Use	The part of your policy that covers any additional expenses if you are unable to live in your home after a loss. See "Additional Living Expense." The amount of coverage is usually 20% of Coverage A.
Coverage E - Personal Liability	The part of your policy that covers your legal responsibility for injuries to your guests.
Coverage F - Medical Payments	The part of your policy that pays medical costs if someone is injured on your property. This is normally $1,000 but can be increased. Anything above the Medical Payments limit would require filing a suit under Coverage E - Personal Liability.
Debris Removal	This covers the cost of removing broken limbs and other debris from an event that causes you to have a loss. For example, a hurricane or tornado knocks over a tree and spreads branches around. This will cover the clean up of that debris.
Deductible	The amount you have to pay per claim before your insurance company will pay.
Endorsement	A change to a policy that can either add coverage or limit coverage. The change can affect many aspects of a policy including who and what is covered. An endorsement may also change the price of your policy.
Exclusion	A type of loss that your policy will not cover.

FAIR	Fair Access to Insurance Requirements. This plan offers fire, windstorm, and hail insurance to people in high-risk areas who might otherwise be denied coverage. This plan is backed by the federal government.
Flood Insurance	A separate policy to protect your property from loss caused by a flood. These policies are issued by the federal government.
Guaranteed Replacement Cost	The value that the insurance company will pay you for a total loss of your home. This means that your home will be repaired to its value at the time of loss regardless of the amount of coverage carried. If you carry coverage of $175,000 on your policy, but it costs $185,000 to rebuild your house, your policy will cover the extra cost. This is not to say that you can carry very low limits on your policy. Your limit must be at least 80% of the replacement cost.
Increased Cost of Construction	A commonly added endorsement to a policy that covers the additional costs of building, repair or reconstruction when you rebuild with more expensive materials and methods required by city ordinances.
Inflation Guard Coverage	An endorsement to the policy that provides automatic increases on the home's insurance to reflect the effects of inflation and increased building costs.
Inland Marine Policy	Broader and more comprehensive coverage that covers property that is limited under the homeowners forms. The coverage can be tailored to meet your needs and there is usually no deductible for this policy. Coverage is provided on a special form (all-risk coverage). Please speak to your agent if you have items that exceed the values provided in your homeowners policy.
Insurance Department	A state agency that monitors insurance company activities in that state. It also assists consumers with insurance issues such as complaints and education.

Liability	A legally enforceable financial obligation.
Negligence	Failure to exercise a generally acceptable level of care and caution.
Policy period	The length of time an insurance policy is valid.
Premium	The amount of money you pay for coverage.
Replacement Cost	The value that the insurance company will pay you for a total loss of your home without deduction for depreciation but limited to a maximum dollar amount. If you carry coverage of $175,000 on your policy but it costs $185,000 to rebuild your house, your policy will only pay up to the $175,000 limit.
Scheduled Property	Property that is described and listed separately on an endorsement to a homeowners, tenants, or unit owners policy. These items have a declared value and do not fall under the Coverage C limit.
Special Form or Special Causes of Loss	Special causes of loss include any cause of loss that is not specifically excluded from the policy. Also known as "all-risk" coverage.